English

1000 SIGHT WORDS MADE EASY

to

I went to school.

now

It's bedtime now.

oxygen

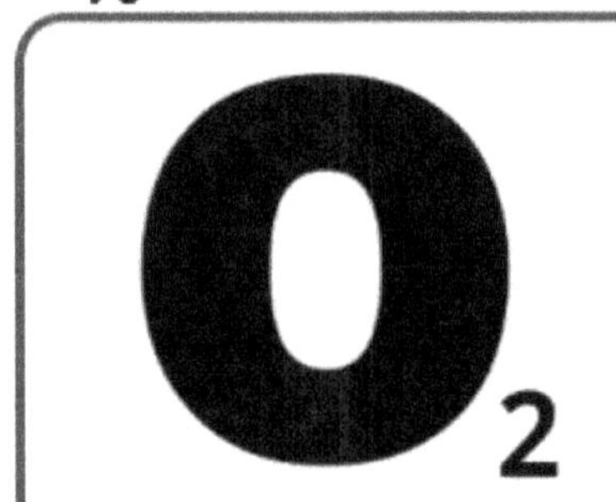

What is the symbol for oxygen?

sail

Do you like to sail?

stay

She knows stay.

about

It's about lunch time.

unit

A centimeter is a unit of length.

fell

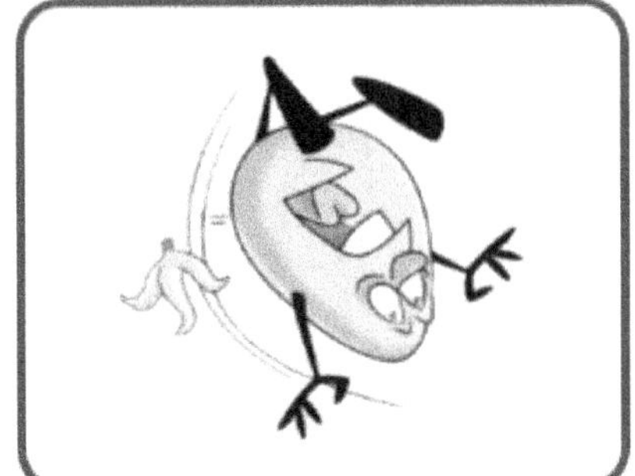

I fell down the stairs.

blue

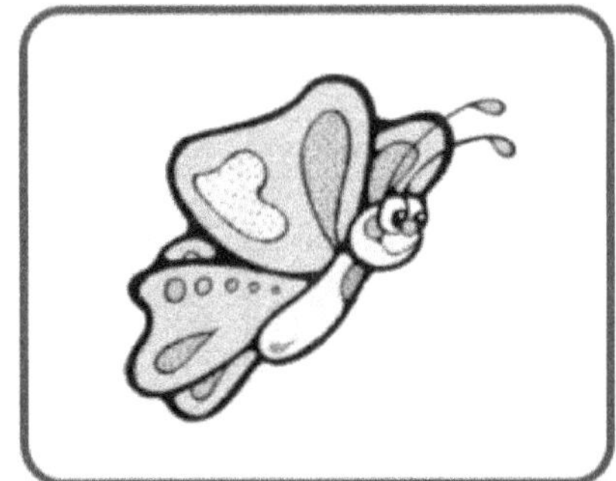

It's a blue butterfly.

coast

The coast is relaxing.

must

You must raise your hand.

british

Who is the British monarch?

remember

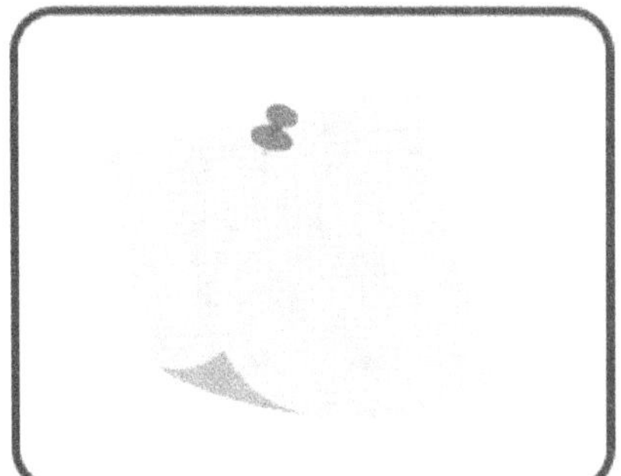

I'll try to remember.

position

She likes sitting in that position.

here

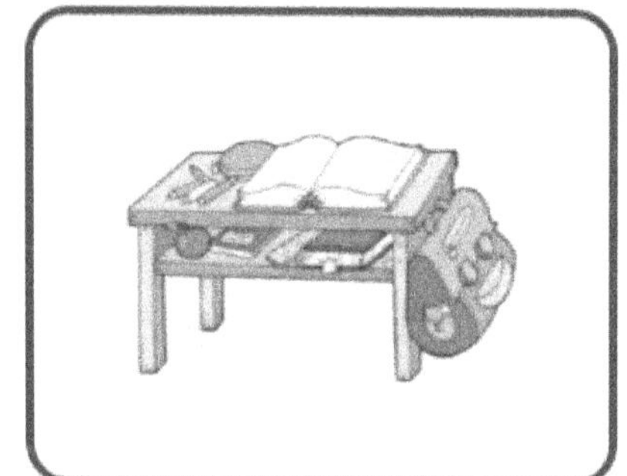

Do you sit here?

exciting

This is so exciting!

color

What is your favorite color?

object

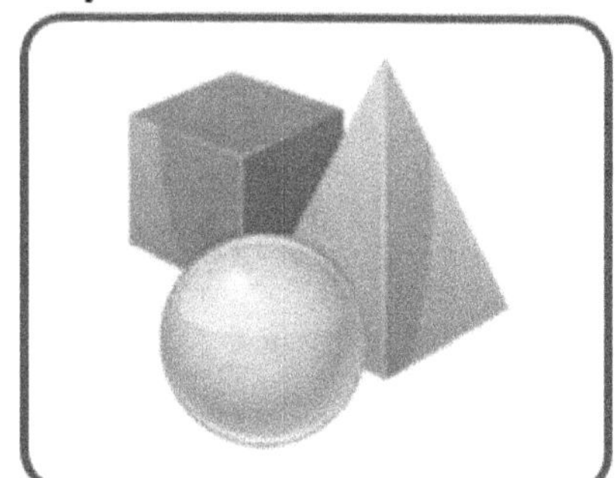

We measured each object.

expect

When do you expect the baby?

may

You may use the computer.

city

He worked in the city.

talk

Let's talk.

wind

The wind is too strong.

bill

Did you receive the bill?

often

How often do you watch tv?

crops

How are the crops growing?

under

It lives under the sea.

life

Life is about friends and family.

copy

Is the copy machine working?

gave

He gave her flowers.

play

Let's play together!

face

They were at the face painting booth.

turn

Turn in your homework.

pole

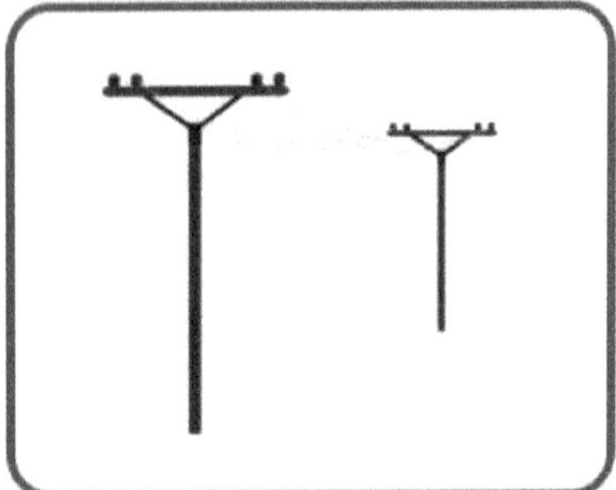

Is that a telephone pole?

do

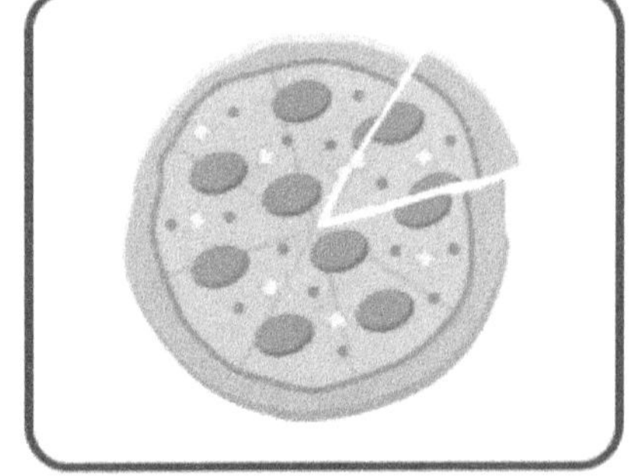

Do you like pizza?

became

She became a nurse.

apple

Eat an apple.

end

She watched to the end.

sure

Sure, I'll go to the magic show!

time

What time is it?

thousands

Thousands of people live here.

who

Who likes hockey?

be

We'll be reading.

live

You live in the city.

statement

He worked on his thesis statement

main

There's the main gate.

test

How'd you do on the test?

hit

They hit up a lot of stores.

bones

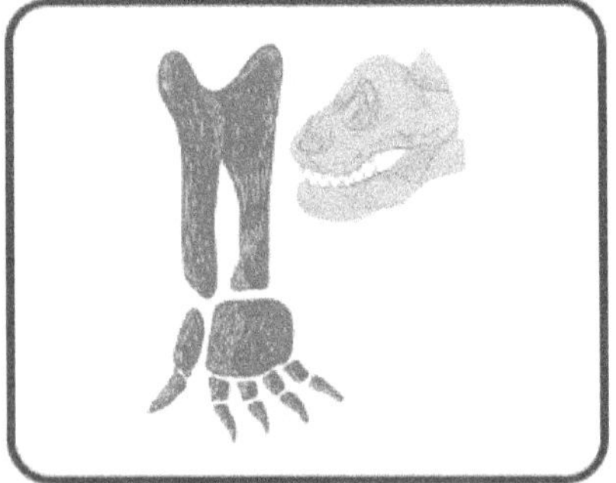

Did you see the dinosaur bones?

mile

It's a mile from here.

brought

Everyone brought a present.

knew

She knew the doctor.

great

Great job!

food

They made a lot of food.

clean

Did you clean?

today

Today we'll go to the pool.

buy

Did you buy a new car?

or

Do you like cats or dogs?

hand

Please hand in your work.

result

What was the result of the election?

hear

You hear through your ears.

list

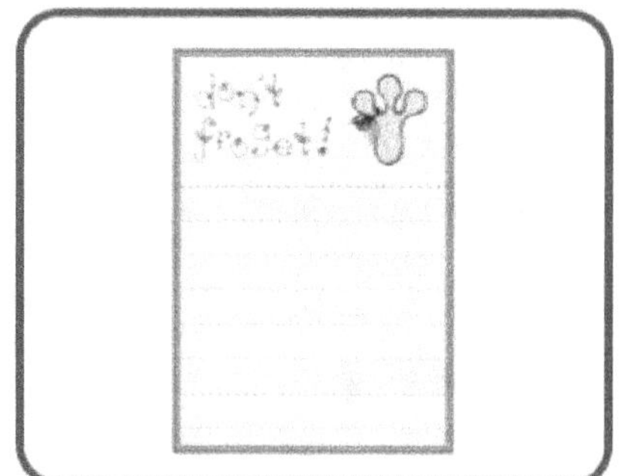

Here's my to-do list

water

Drink more water.

picked

They picked the book together.

case

Don't forget your case.

doctor

He went to see the doctor.

it's

It's a tiger cub.

europe

Are you going to visit Europe?

saw

We saw a UFO.

finally

She finally smiled.

step

Here's the step ladder.

lifted

The jeep is lifted.

repeated

They repeated the exercises daily.

everyone

Everyone was working.

thick

That's a thick book.

bell

Ring the bell.

maybe

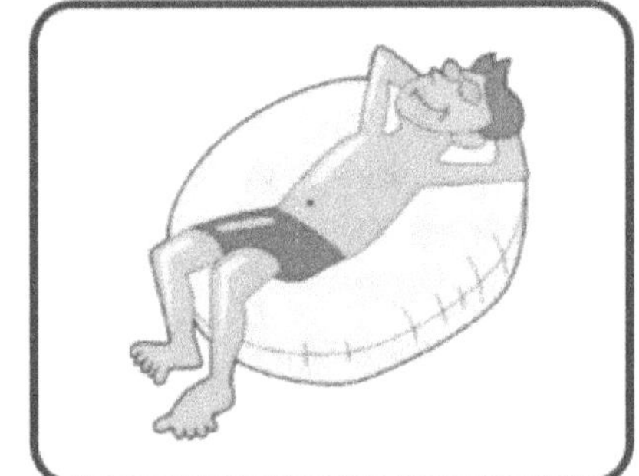

Maybe we'll go rafting.

products

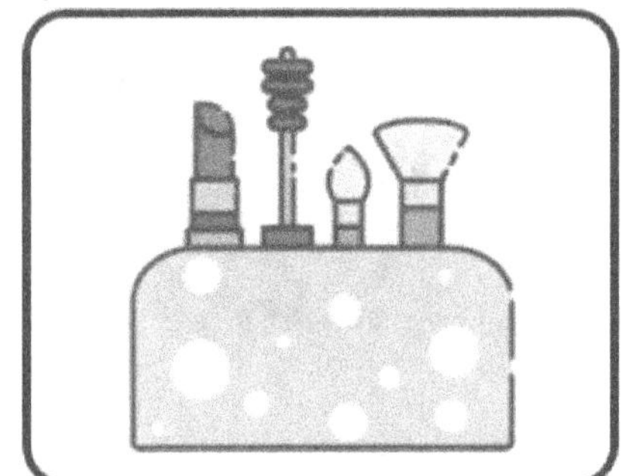

Which products do you like?

action

Action!

filled

It's filled with flowers.

weather

What is the weather like?

save

Try to save some money.

hold

Hold on to the balloons!

plan

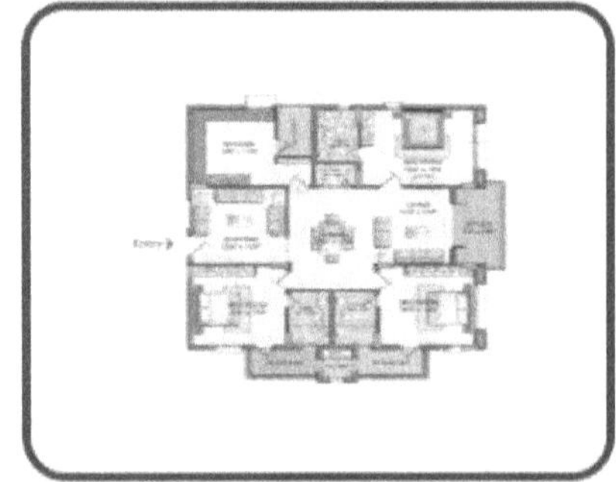

Look at the house plan.

hot

The coffee is hot.

above

The sky was above them.

them

I invited them to my party.

president

Make sure you vote for president

rhythm

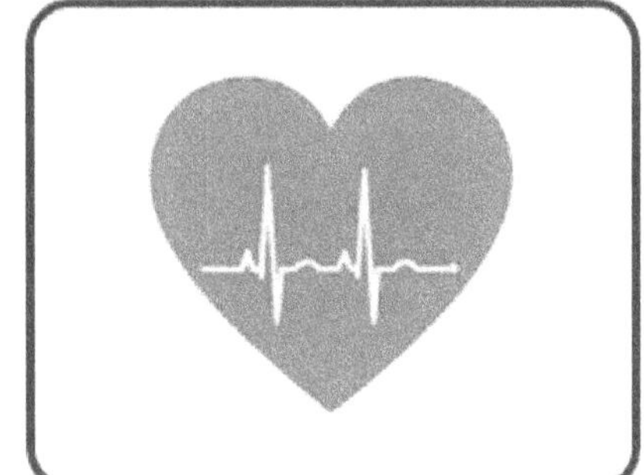

That's your heart's rhythm.

wear

Did you find a suit to wear?

hard

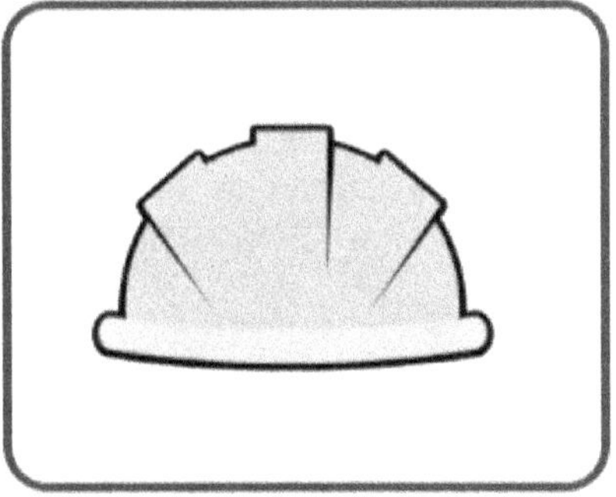

He wore a hard hat.

during

We learn a lot during class.

dollars

How many hundreds of dollars is it?

south

Mexico is south of the US.

front

She was at the front of the line.

settled

The case was settled.

please

Please have breakfast.

desert

Have you been to the desert?

suddenly

It happened suddenly.

melody

What a beautiful melody.

on

Please turn on the light.

column

Did you read the newspaper column?

field

It's the new football field.

tiny

It's so tiny.

almost

It's almost lunch time.

street

It's on this street.

amount

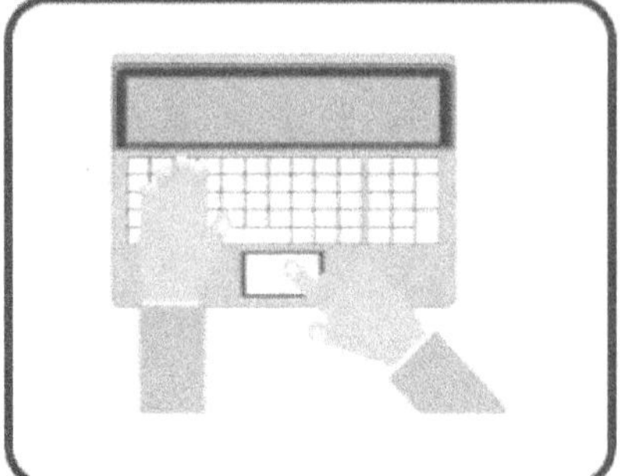

What amount of work do you have left?

our

She was our teacher.

died

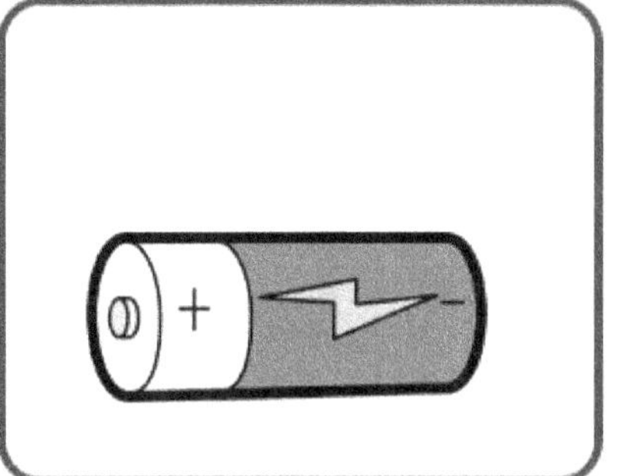

I didn't charge my phone and it died.

center

The bullseye is the center.

special

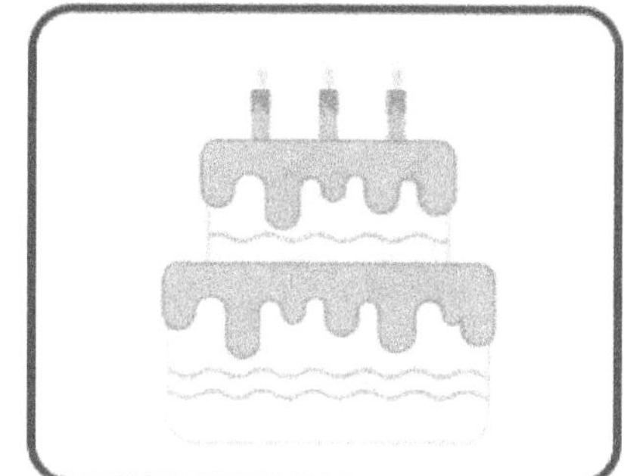

It's a special cake.

king

Have you ever met a king?

one

There is one cupcake left.

fraction

What fraction of the cake did you eat?

down

We walked down the stairs.

begin

You may begin your exam.

score

What was the final score?

wide

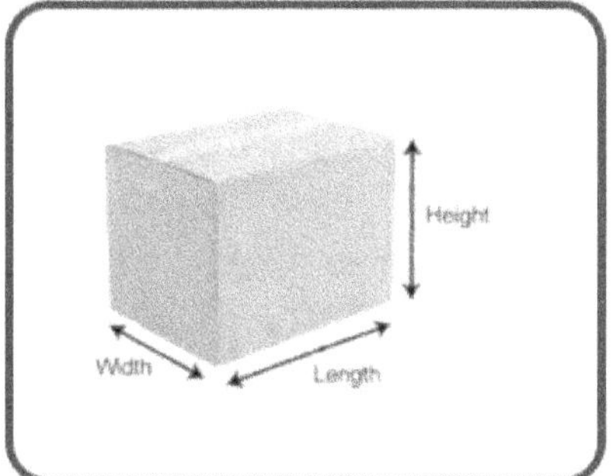

How wide is the box?

class

It's a class party.

felt

He felt happy with friends.

bad

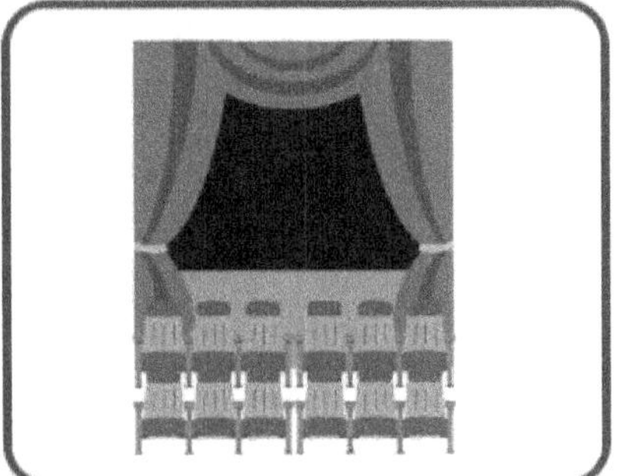

The movie was bad.

branches

There are three branches.

river

The river is high.

hair

Did you get get your hair cut?

appear

You appear to be lost.

wife

His wife is a teacher.

before

Sharpen your pencil before the test.

wash

We decided to wash the car.

been

I've been to Mexico.

more

I need more time.

similar

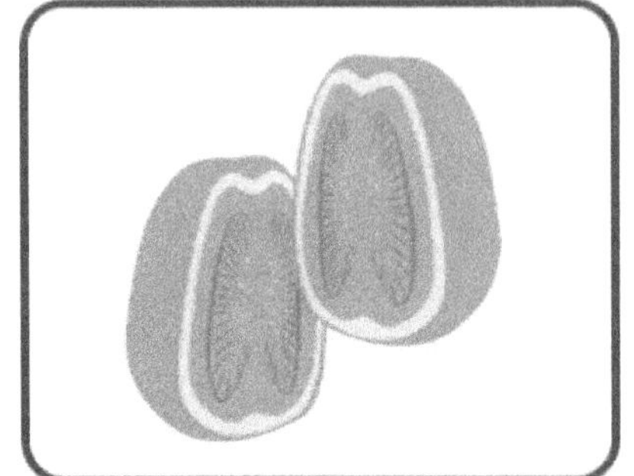

The halves are similar.

upon

Once upon a time there was a princess.

come

Will you come to the park?

woman

The woman was on her way to work.

choose

Which one did you choose?

deal

Did you agree on the deal?

paragraph

Have you written a paragraph?

fine

He had to pay a fine.

birds

There's a lot of birds.

however

He hates milk, however he drank it.

little

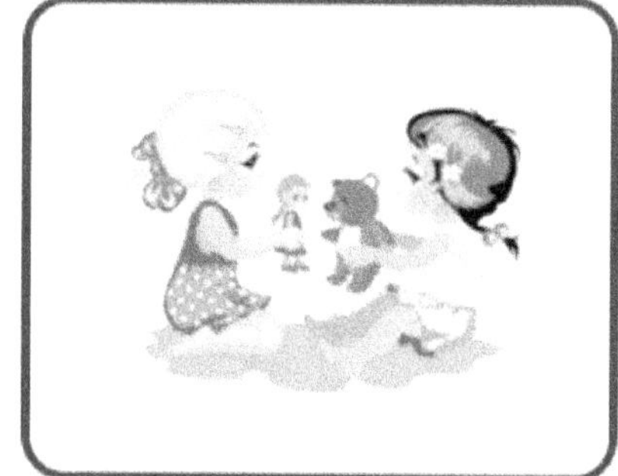

He has a little sister.

began

The baby began to cry.

rise

We were waiting for the sun to rise.

suppose

I suppose we could go to the pool.

cut

You use scissors to cut.

only

There's only one slice left.

pounds

The price was in pounds.

a

A girl sang.

arrived

My plane arrived on time.

particular

I prefer a particular ketchup.

possible

Will it be possible to grill this weekend?

tree

Did you decorate the tree?

track

The runners got on the track.

experiment

What was your experiment?

seat

The girls took a seat in the sand.

sent

Was the email sent?

you're

You're an angel.

run

He likes to run with his dog.

new

We have a new teacher.

close

Please close the door.

snow

Let's play in the snow!

represent

He drew pictures to represent words.

square

A square has four equal sides.

four

There were four of them.

fast

A cheetah is fast.

very

He is a very good singer.

block

Did you have a toy block?

train

We have a Christmas train.

left

Are you left or right handed?

vowel

What are vowels?

metal

They have a metal trashcan.

sigh

Did you sigh?

winter

Winter is here!

after

You may have dessert after dinner.

part

He ate part of my homework.

increase

Did the house value increase?

the

The weather is nice.

fly

Did you fly there?

surface

Most of the Earth's surface is water.

several

They looked at several creatures.

own

Do you own a computer?

shoes

Put your shoes on.

simple

It was a simple dress.

sound

A bee makes a buzzing sound.

miss

You may correct any you miss.

student

The students worked together

chief

Is your dad the fire chief?

business

They opened their business.

soldiers

They are soldiers.

sugar

Sugar cube for your tea?

some

I need some paper.

start

Start writing.

strange

That's strange looking.

molecules

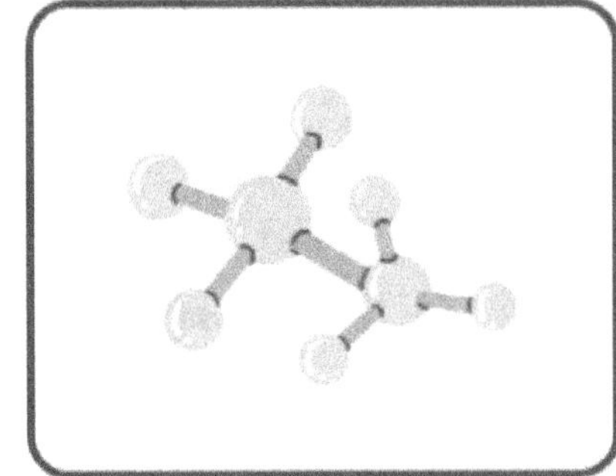

Are those molecules?

triangle

How many sides does a triangle have?

take

Please take your seat.

both

They both worked on math.

mouth

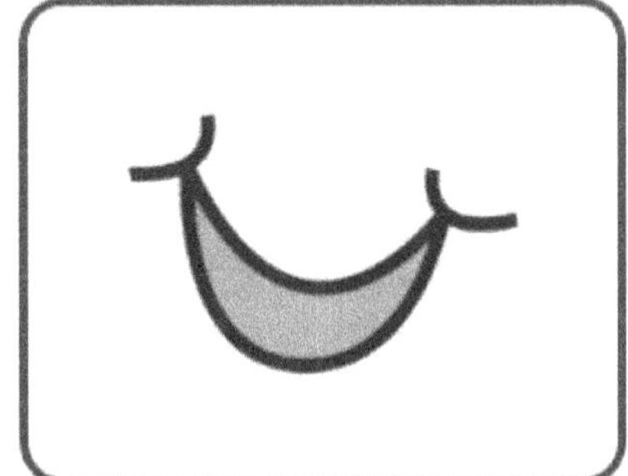

Do your braces make your mouth hurt?

heart

Did you draw a heart?

most

Most students like to help.

sentence

Complete the sentence.

west

You need to go west.

march

Are you going to march with the band?

speak

Who will speak next?

animal

My favorite animal is a lion.

america

Columbus sailed to America.

hill

The sun peaked over the hill.

draw

Do you like to draw?

legs

A cricket has six legs.

still

I still want ice skates.

too

Do you like chocolate too?

difficult

I found this difficult.

art

Do you like to look at art?

area

There are no wild animals in this area.

experience

She has a lot of experience.

shape

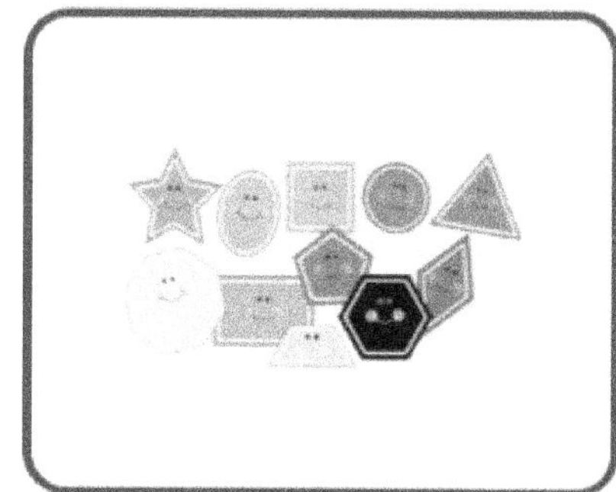

What shape is that?

factors

What are the factors of these numbers?

meet

Do you want to meet them?

value

The value of family is greater.

can

Can you go to the zoo?

made

You made an A on the test.

church

Did you go to church?

of

I'm proud of you!

wait

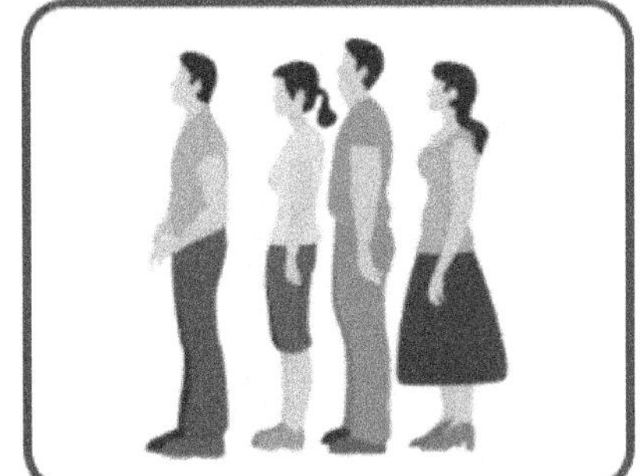

How long did you wait?

room

They hang out in this room.

company

What company do you work for?

gas

We stopped to get gas.

go

May we go to recess?

bright

The sun is really bright.

country

Do you live in the country?

compare

You can't compare apples to oranges.

poor

Did you do poor on the exam?

when

When is the dance?

board

That's her surf board

plural

What is the plural of a mouse?

number

Her jersey number is twelve.

along

We get along.

did

Did you buy popcorn?

total

What's the total?

passed

She passed her driver's exam.

six

He rolled a six.

there

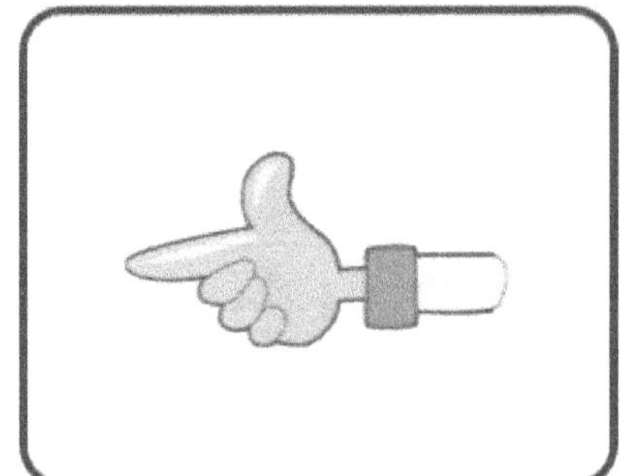

It's over there.

we

We went to the beach.

surprise

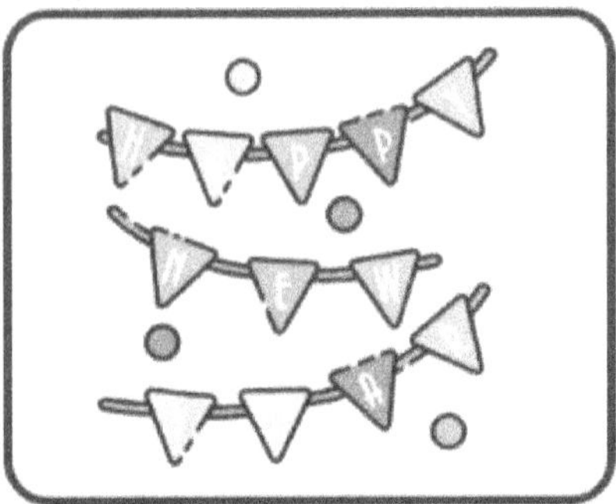

She threw a surprise party.

party

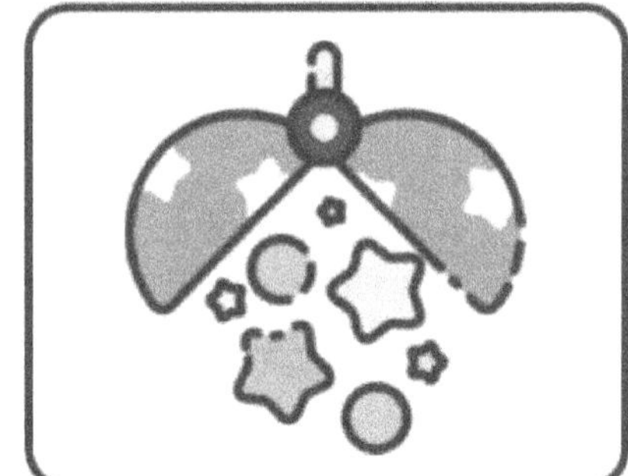

How was the party?

good

The hamburger was good.

period

You put a period at the end.

big

The elephant is a big animal.

quiet

Quiet in the library.

called

I need to call my mom

hunting

We're hunting for Easting eggs.

details

Look for the details.

themselves

They enjoyed themselves.

black

He has a black cat.

oh

Oh! It's a puppy!

energy

Have you used solar energy?

instruments

What instruments do you play?

else

Did you draw that or did someone else?

known

They've known each other forever.

sun

The sun was out.

hope

Let's hope.

show

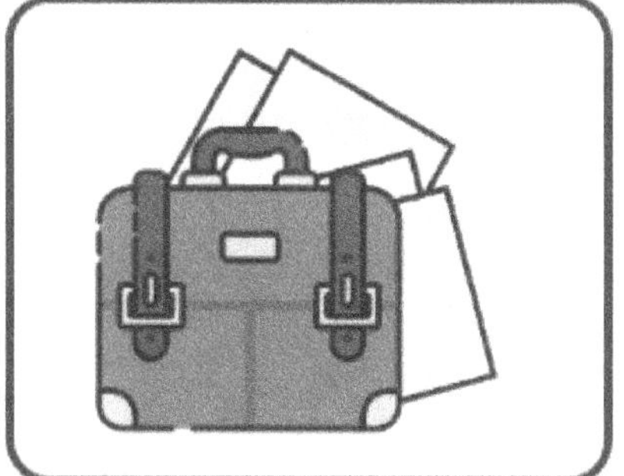

Show your work.

division

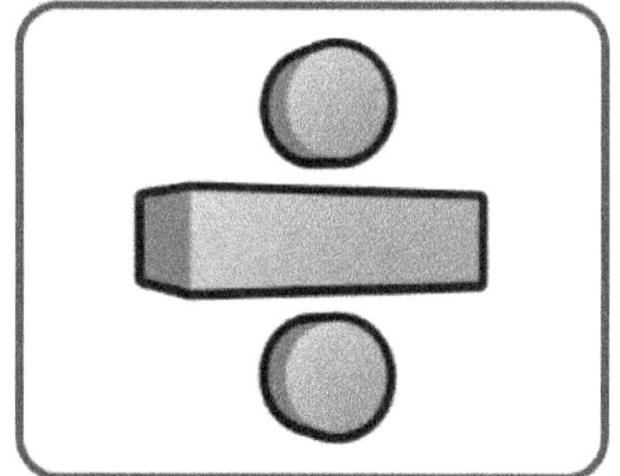

We did division today.

woman

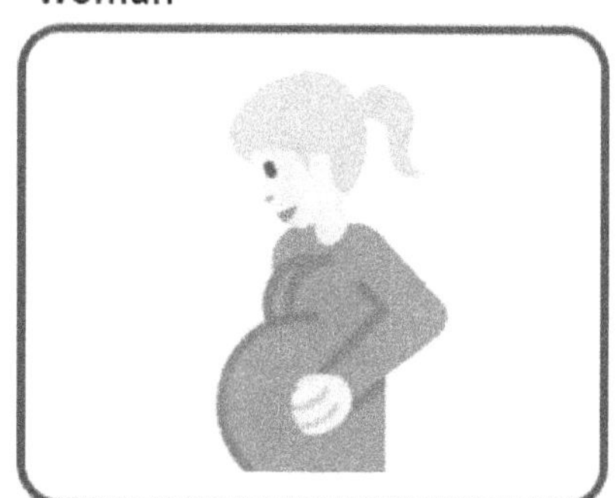

Is the woman pregnant?

ten

Did you hit all ten pins?

had

Mrs. Smith had a cold.

science

We love science.

god

Many believe in God and angels.

fact

Is that a fact or opinion?

use

Let's use the pool.

wheels

Did you buy new wheels?

army

Is he joining the army?

system

Tell me about the solar system.

evening

The ceremony was this evening.

exercise

We all should exercise.

page

Please turn the page.

smiled

He always smiled

many

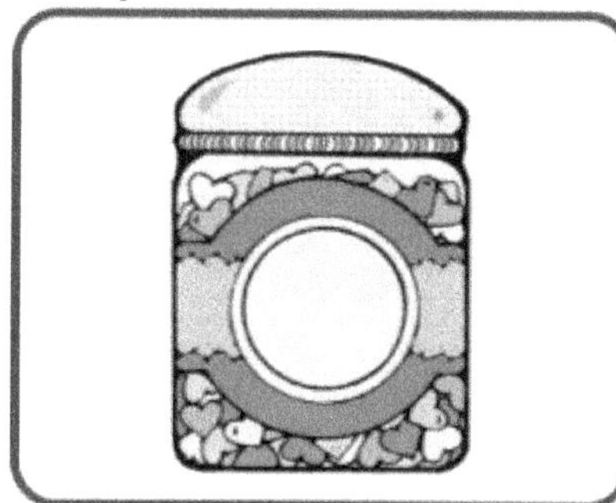

How many are in the jar?

soon

Dinner will be ready soon.

red

It's a red heart.

except

like all vegetables except peas.

members

All the members were there.

dictionary

You may use a dictionary.

at

You're at school.

northern

He lives in northern California.

mountains

There are alot of mountains here.

but

I like peas, but not cabbage.

rather

I'd rather be reading.

common

They have a lot in common.

noun

Is that a noun or a verb?

include

They made sure to include sunscreen.

fresh

All the fruit is fresh.

nothing

He had nothing he had to do.

report

Your report card looks great!

town

Meet at the town square.

whether

Whether you go by bus or not, go.

joined

I joined them at the cafe.

captain

Who is the ship's captain?

sign

There's a stop sign.

skin

She used a mask for her skin.

need

Do you need to sleep?

ground

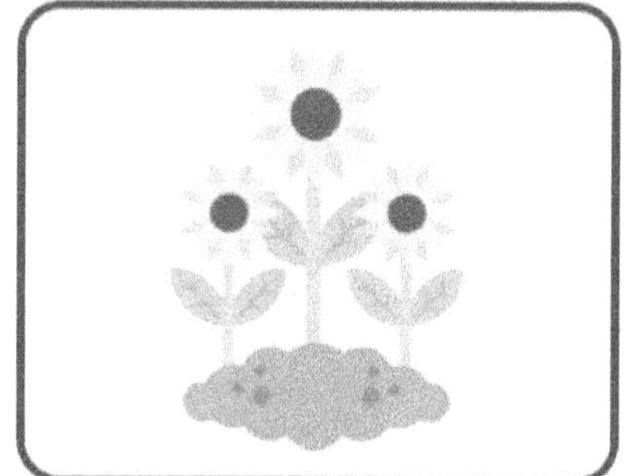

Grass covered the ground.

straight

It's a straight road.

happened

What happend?

air

The air was cold.

reached

You reached high for your goals.

record

Who broke the record?

beside

They stood beside one another.

oil

I changed the oil in my car.

does

Does he ride the bus?

let's

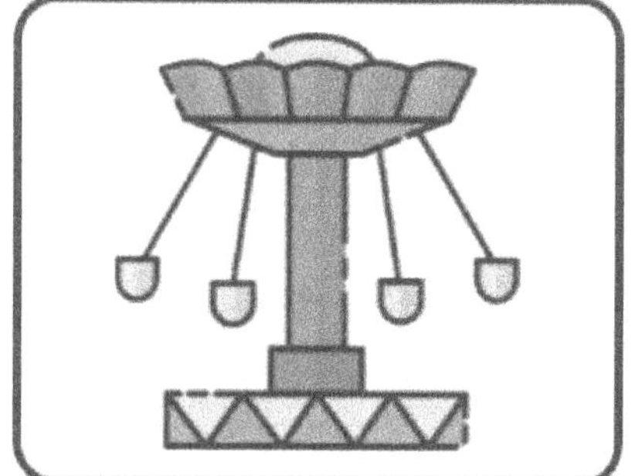

Let's go to the fair!

bed

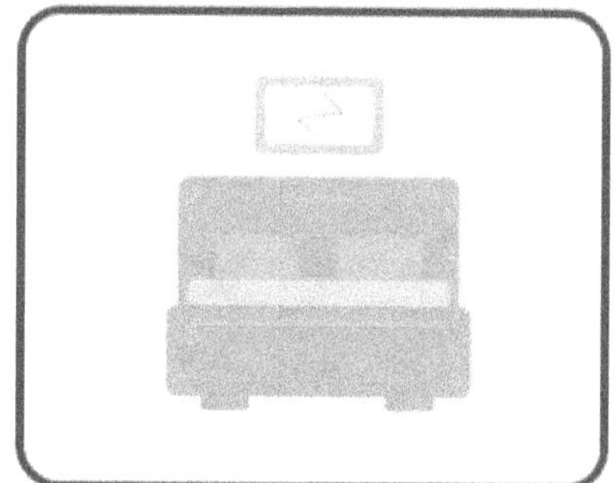

We have a bunk bed.

island

The island was beautiful.

loud

The concert is loud.

store

What store did you go to?

east

Are you from the east coast?

leave

He packed to leave.

learn

It's fun to learn science.

full

The basket was full.

france

Have you ever been to France?

wings

She was flapping her wings.

tone

He said he's tone deaf.

near

We are near the beach.

flow

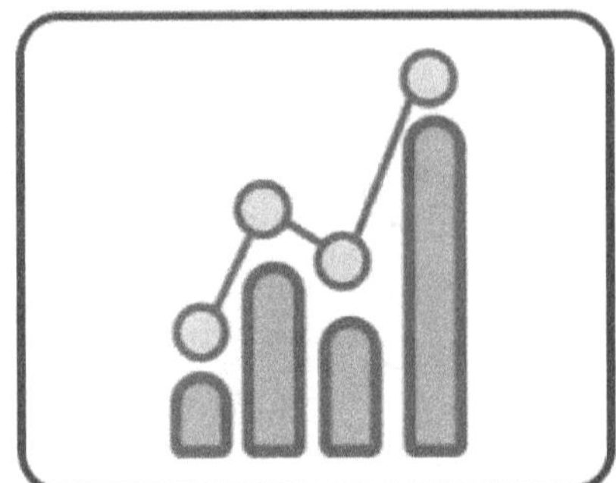

We created a flow chart.

wrote

She wrote poetry

actually

I actually like strawberry.

finished

He finished his painting.

ever

Don't ever doubt yourself!

course

Did you go to the golf course?

we'll

We'll finish buying our groceries.

brother

Is that your brother?

change

I save my change.

underline

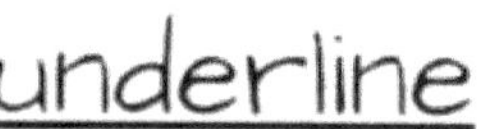

Underline the word.

waves

The waves were great for surfing.

ship

The ship sailed.

lake

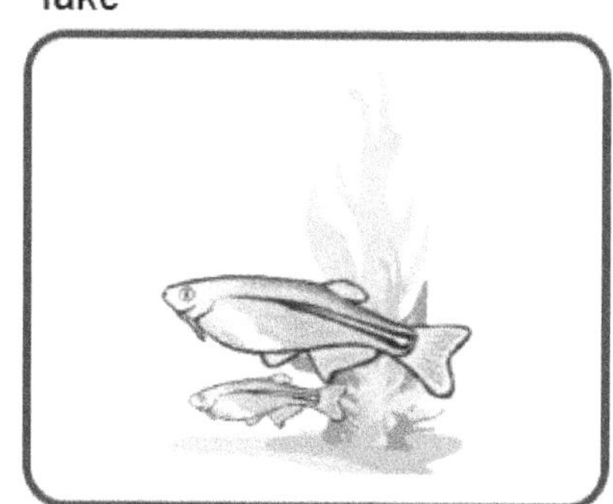

We're still going to the lake.

look

Let's look at the stars.

every

I shower every day.

developed

They developed a strong friendship.

example

This is an example of a bird.

japanese

These are Japanese cherry blossoms.

day

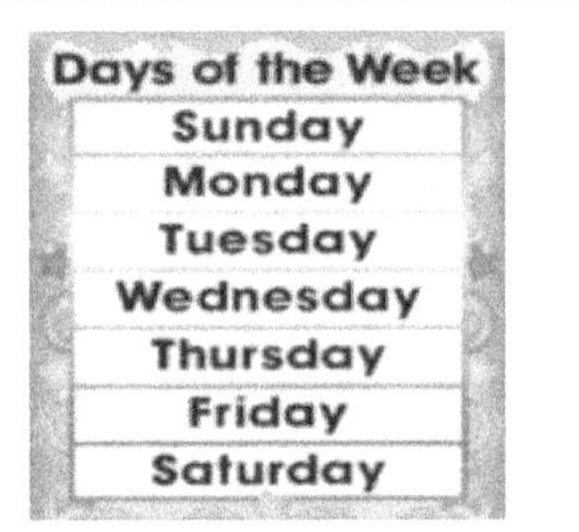

What day is it today?

past

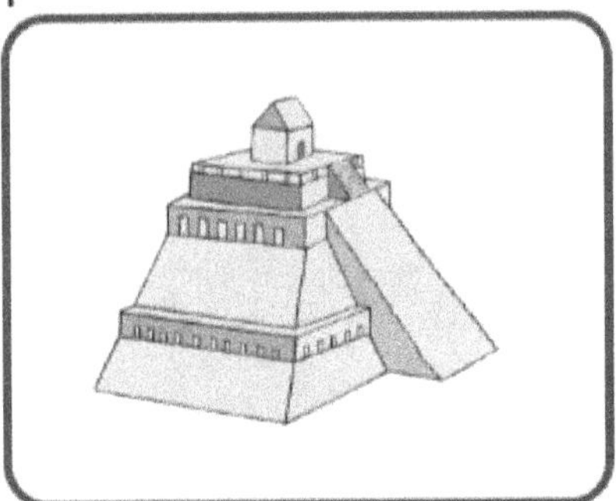

Archeology looks at the past.

stone

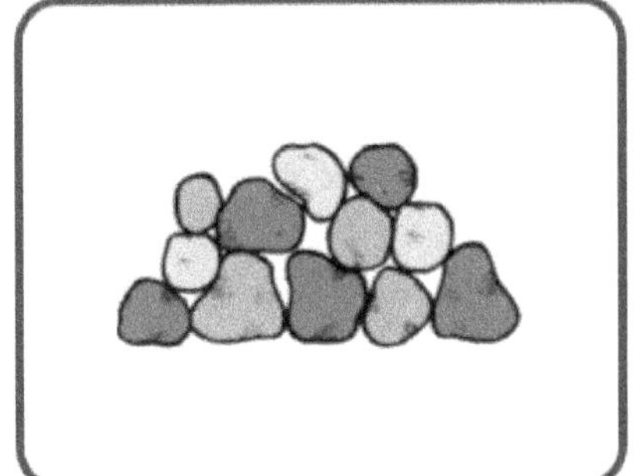

She skipped a stone across the pond.

never

I've never broken my leg.

himself

He smiled to himself.

touch

The cheerleader can touch her toes

bottom

There's treasure at the bottom.

friends

They are my friends.

level

Use the level to hang the picture.

serve

Did you serve that table?

bought

She bought new clothes.

answer

Raise your hand to answer.

because

I went to bed because I was tired.

third

How did you like third grade?

bank

I need to go to the bank

death

The grim reaper is death.

although

Although sunny, it's cold out.

always

She always brushes her teeth.

act

Do you like to act in a play?

corn

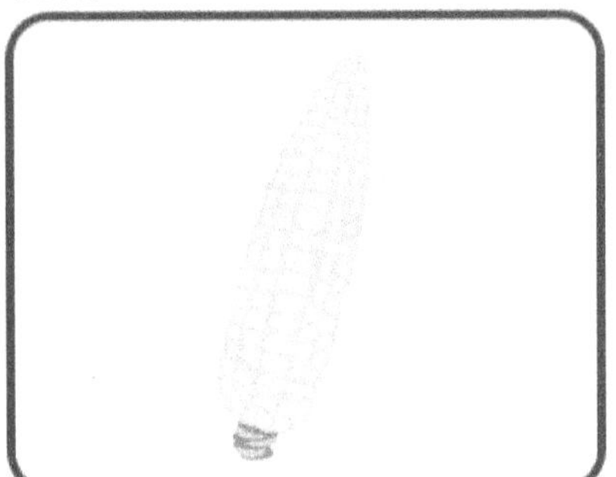

Do you like corn?

spring

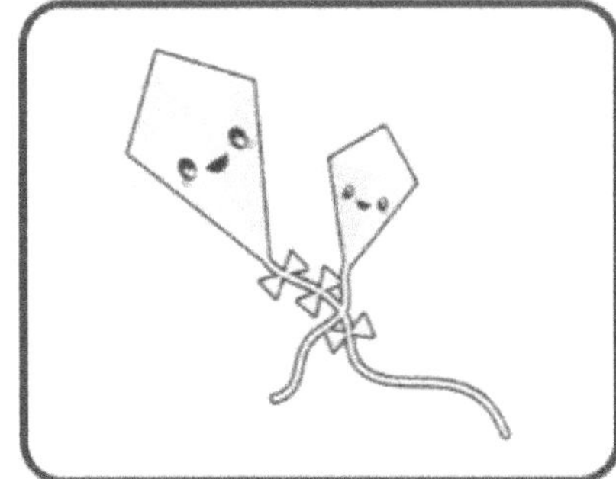

Is it finally spring?

catch

Did you catch the ball?

best

Do your best!

words

You make words to play.

property

That property is for sale.

radio

Let's listen to the radio.

which

Which snack do you want?

string

It's a red string.

interesting

The dog thought the toy was interesting.

french

She's a French bull dog.

should

We should exercise.

off

The rocket blasted off.

cannot

You cannot succeed without hard work.

things

She washed a lot of things.

say

What did you say?

matter

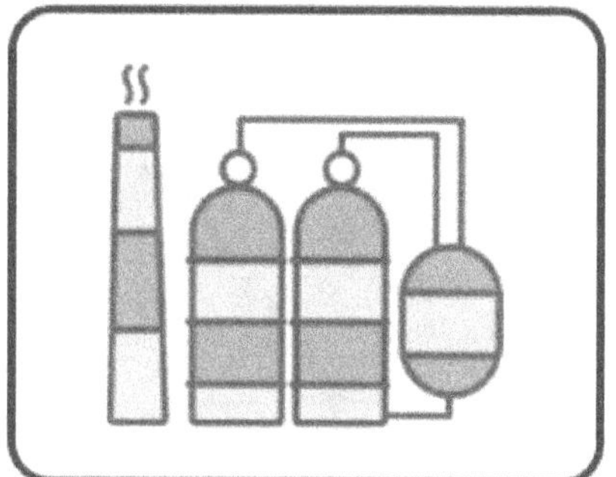

What are the states of matter?

wasn't

Wasn't that your cousin?

safe

Do you have a safe?

engine

The fire engine parked there.

suffix

What is the suffix of the word?

soil

Plant it in the soil.

decimal

Where does the decimal go?

yes

Yes, I want to go.

clear

The glass is clear.

rolled

The diploma was rolled up.

greek

Have you ever had Greek food?

happy

Music made him happy.

flowers

Flowers are growing there.

factories

There are a lot of factories there.

right

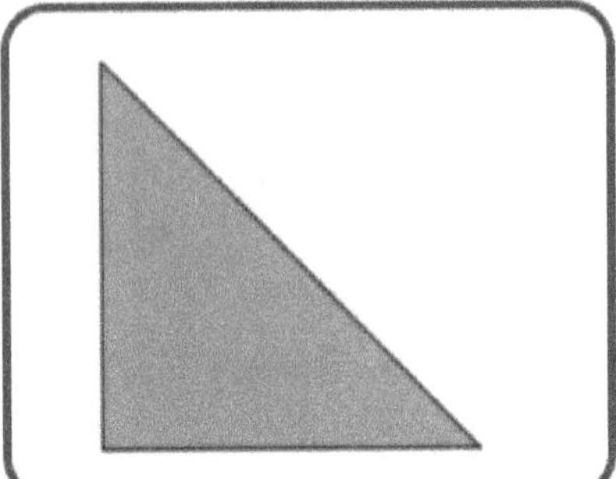

That's a right triangle.

grass

Will you cut the grass?

she

She had fun with her friends.

solve

Did you solve the equation?

dark

It's dark at night.

difference

What's the difference?

dry

Try to stay dry.

up

We walked up the stairs.

electric

Do you own an electric car?

over

He jumped over it.

continued

He continued to look through the box.

consider

Did you consider it?

in

Halloween is in October.

mind

Your mind is full of imagination.

rule

Which rule did you break?

cool

That's a cool car.

heavy

It's really heavy.

second

She won second place.

divided

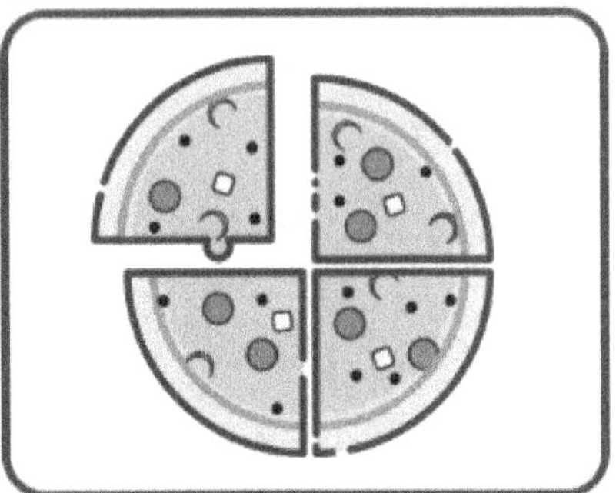

It was divided up.

either

Will either of you wash the car?

interest

I have an interest in flowers.

her

It is her doll.

way

It's a one way street.

am

I am hungry.

boy

The boy played a basketball.

low

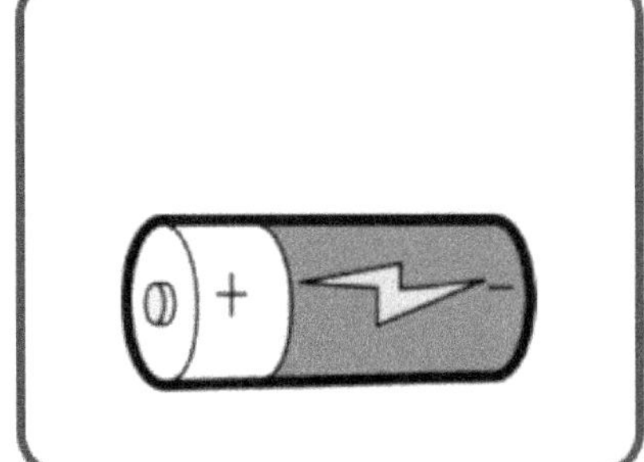

My battery is low.

think

Think about it.

history

She taught history.

move

His family decided to move.

plane

Is it your first time on a plane?

seen

Have any of you seen the movie?

complete

Did you complete your workout?

travel

Let's travel.

stream

We played at the stream.

know

I don't know.

determine

Did you determine where to go eat?

afraid

What are you afraid of?

blood

I donated blood.

everything

Everything here is fun.

these

These are my markers.

beat

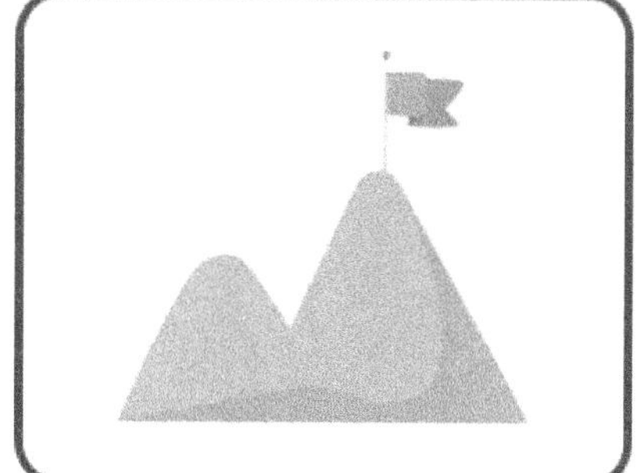

Our team beat yours.

drive

Does your dad drive you?

valley

They traveled to the valley.

adjective

Tell me an adjective to describe this.

white

They drew on the white board.

spot

It's a red spot.

cattle

We raise cattle.

easy

He thought it was easy.

why

She asked why?

shall

I shall ride this.

rope

Do you have any rope?

thin

That's a thin book.

have

Do you have a pencil?

fish

Do you like fish?

milk

Did you drink your milk?

numeral

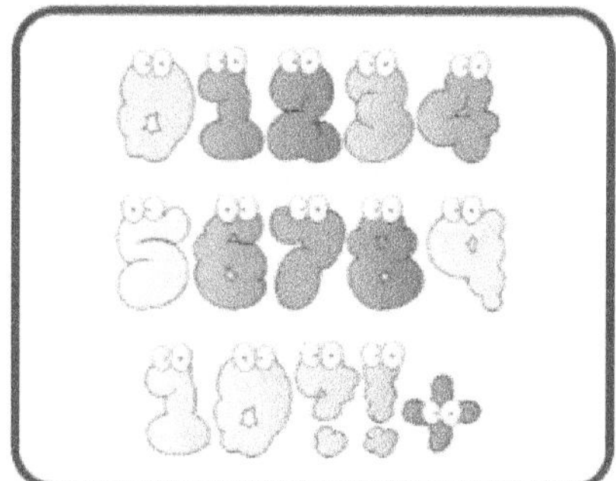

Which numeral did you choose?

below

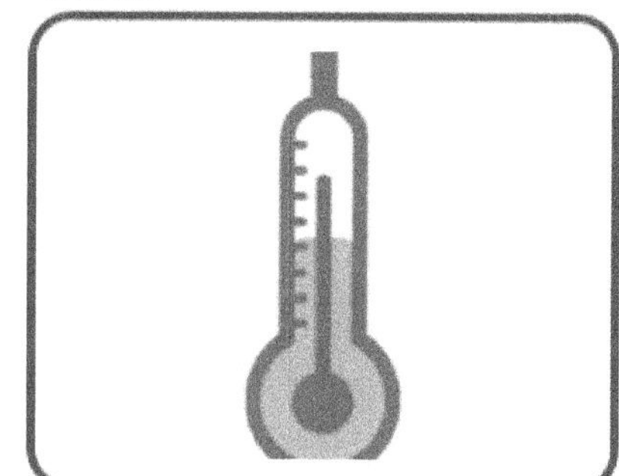

It's below thirty degrees.

much

How much is the camera?

late

You're late.

smell

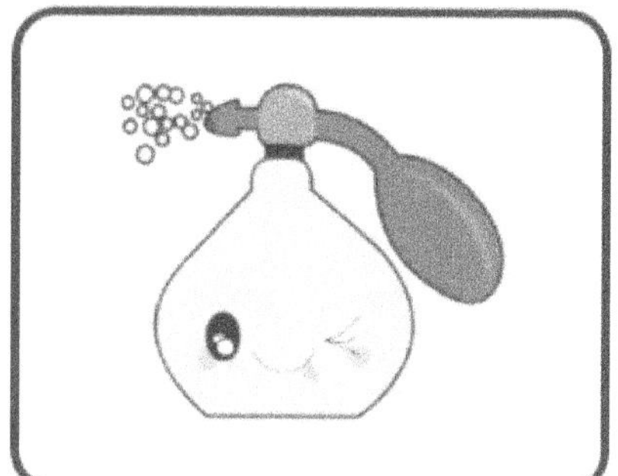

I love the smell of cookies!

believe

I believe in Santa Claus.

cook

What did you cook?

land

They bought some land.

people

Alot of people were dancing.

tube

That's my tube of toothpaste.

even

They learned about even numbers.

game

Who won the game?

hundred

She made a one hundred on the quiz.

weight

The scale will measure your weight.

build

What are you going to build?

order

Put them in order of date.

trade

I'll trade you my sandwich for yours.

uncle

We learned about Uncle Sam.

shown

The photo was shown to me.

rest

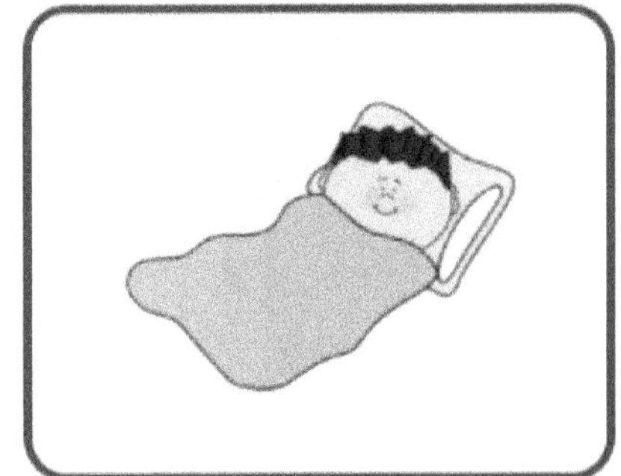

You needed to rest.

name

What is his name?

forest

Where is the forest?

done

Well done!

home

Is this your home?

large

A bear is large.

someone

Someone cleaned their desk.

ring

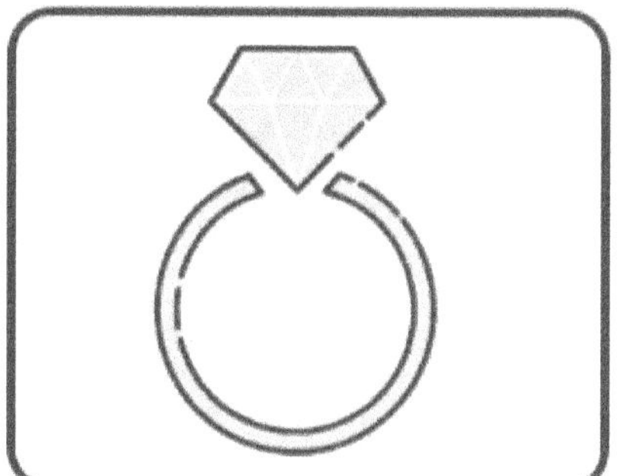

Such a beautiful ring!

forward

Spring forward the clocks.

sharp

Those are sharp scissors.

single

A single balloon

didn't

I didn't know.

addition

Do you learn addition?

flight

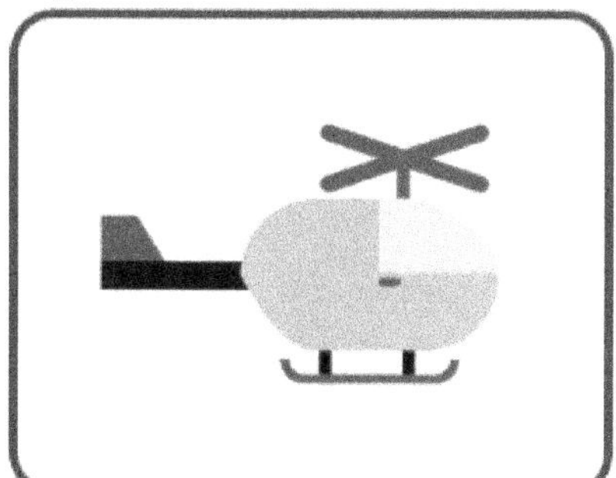

The helicopter took flight.

entire

The entire family was in the picture.

age

They were around the same age

different

They use different balls.

found

We found a puppy.

printed

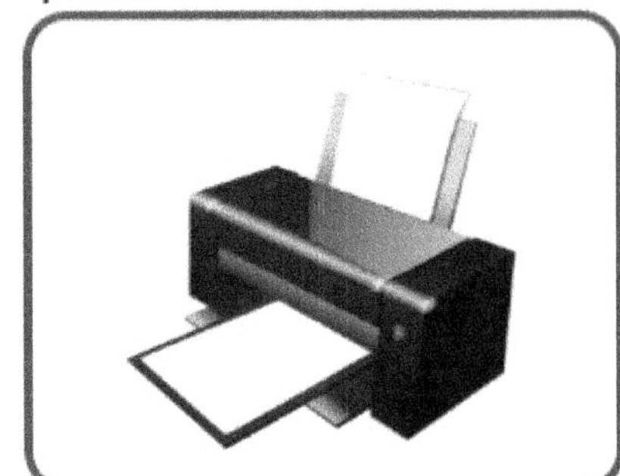

She printed out the forms.

no

No talking in the library.

garden

She worked in the garden

yellow

A banana is yellow.

necessary

It is necessary to go to school.

equal

Does it equal four?

inside

He was inside the dog house.

earth

Our planet is Earth.

job

What job did you chose?

substances

What are these substances?

questions

Do you have questions?

information

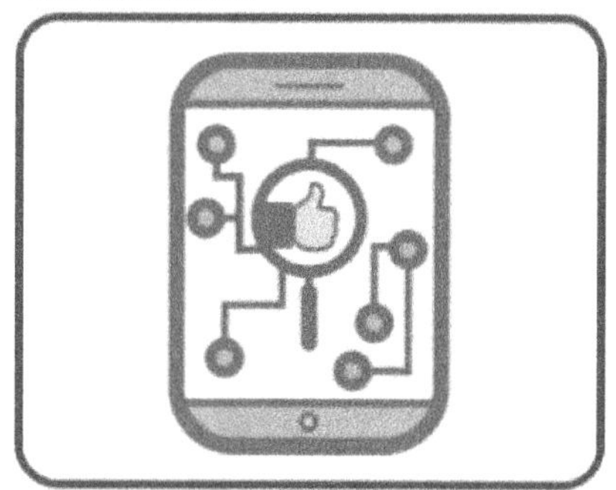

He took in so much information.

consonant

What is the consonant?

green

The frog is green.

cried

She cried.

check

Did you get a check mark?

horse

Have you ever ridden a horse?

reason

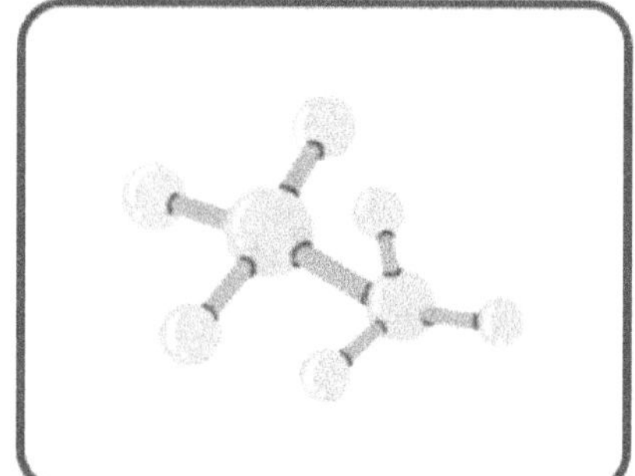

Science uses logic and reason.

race

The race is about to begin.

first

He earned first place.

fear

I have a huge fear of clowns.

father

Her father walked her to school.

heard

I heard you like music.

outside

They brought sand in from outside.

win

Did you win?

won't

Won't you go fishing with me?

pay

We need to pay

site

Have you looked at the site?

pulled

He pulled the wagon.

fire

We made a fire.

village

We travled to the village.

same

Did you get the same answer?

person

He's a smart person.

yard

Lucky is in the yard.

i

I like icecream.

north

Go north.

ocean

I love the ocean.

against

It's against the rules.

cotton

A q-tip is made of cotton.

you

You are strong.

three

It's the number three.

lead

We were in the lead.

present

Who is the present for?

fair

Let's go to the fair.

planets

We were learning about the planets.

meat

Do you eat meat?

that

That is my house.

speed

What's the speed limit?

cells

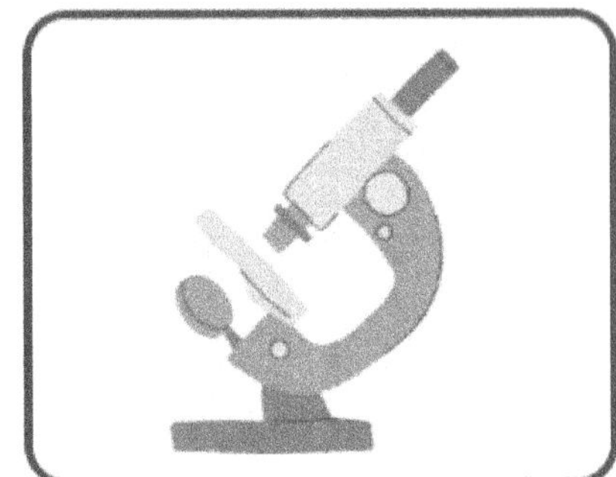

We learned about cells.

round

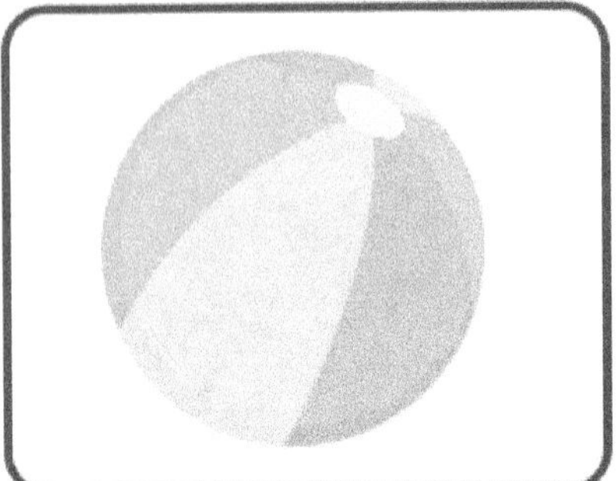

The soccer ball is round.

fingers

Cross your fingers.

crowd

There was a large crowd.

it

It is raining.

kept

She kept hold of the balloon.

human

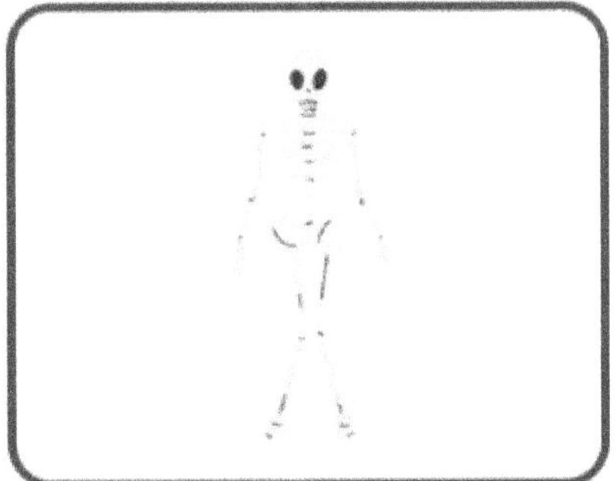

We learned about the human body.

family

How big is your family?

foot

Twelve inches is a foot.

phrase

His phrase inlcuded a penny.

child

The child prayed.

pattern

Which dress pattern?

group

They were working in a group.

wish

Make a wish!

said

She said hello.

insects

Do you like insects?

and

I like cats and dogs.

work

Hard work pays off.

circle

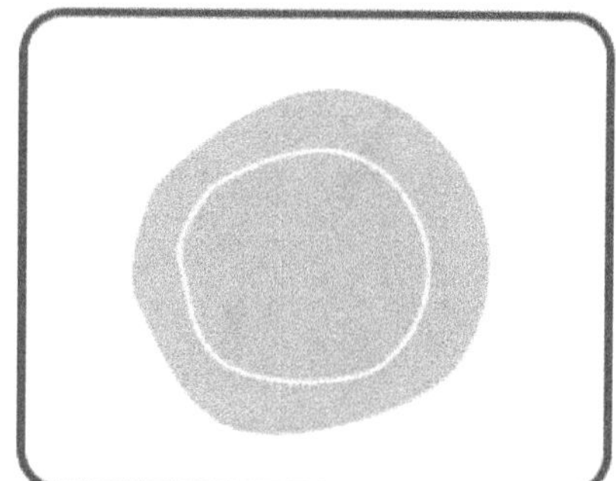

She drew a circle.

notice

Put the notice on the board.

exactly

It was exactly as she imagined.

from

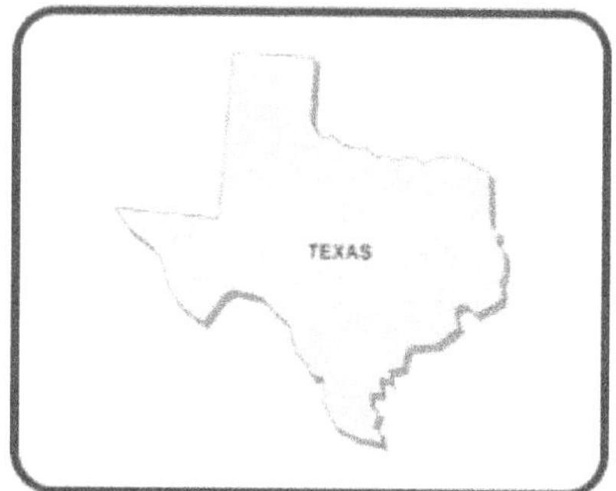

I am from Texas.

write

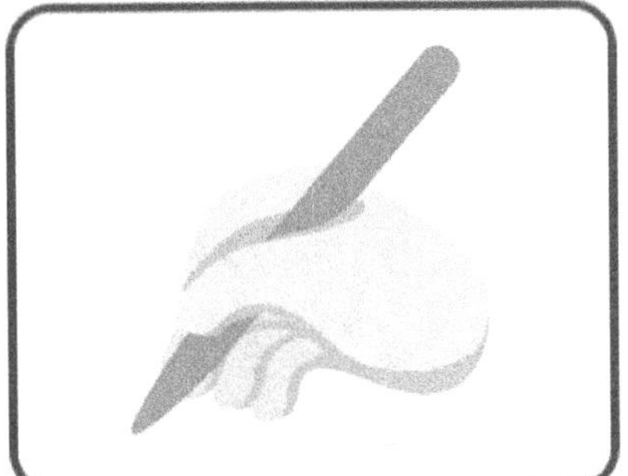

Please write your name.

certain

Certain words are harder than others.

body

The body has a lot of bones.

moment

Wait a moment for the bus.

measure

Did you measure it?

pair

Are those your pair of shoes?

flat

The tire was flat.

sometimes

Sometimes we watch tv.

mine

Be mine.

find

Did you find your keys?

note

She left a note.

read

Do you like to read?

row

Did you go out on row boats?

through

He was through with the race.

lost

Have you lost something?

trip

Did you enjoy your road trip?

away

Throw your trash away.

bit

I bit the apple.

morning

Do you drink coffee in the morning?

key

Did you find your key?

terms

Did you learn new vocabulary terms?

farmers

Farmers work hard.

problem

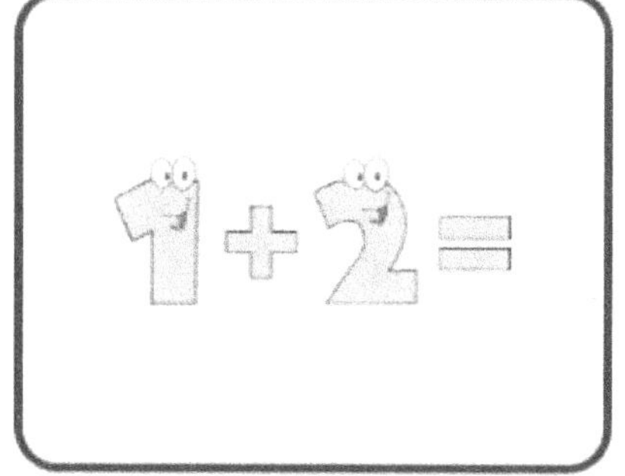

Let's solve the problem.

war

The war of the Empire and the Republic.

warm	**fit**	**swim**

How warm is the soup?	How much did you fit in there?	Let's go for a swim!
indian	**arms**	**killed**

It's an Indian elephant.	She crossed her arms.	Pest control killed the bugs.
men	**laughed**	**also**

The men played football.	They all laughed.	I also like baseball.
girl	**see**	**seeds**

The girl wore pink shoes.	He can't see without glasses.	Did you get seeds for the garden?

ran

They ran the race.

dead

The bug is dead.

place

This is my favorite place.

solution

I figured out a solution!

alone

While alone, he read.

drop

Did you drop and crack it?

eight

Did you hit the eight ball?

floor

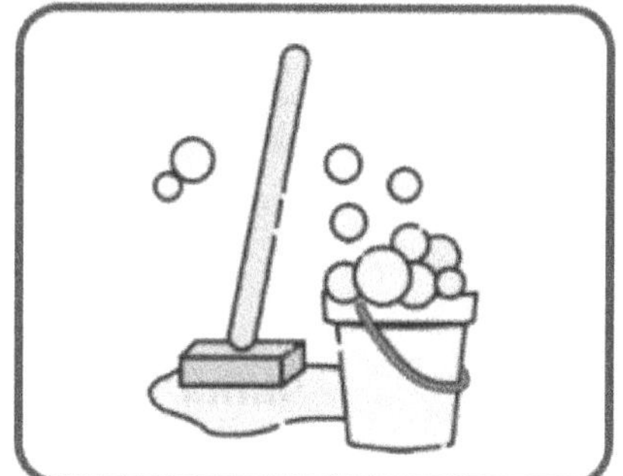

Did you mop the floor?

across

It's across the street.

quickly

The greyhound ran quickly.

behind

The cow was behind the fence.

understand

Do you understand the homework?

equation

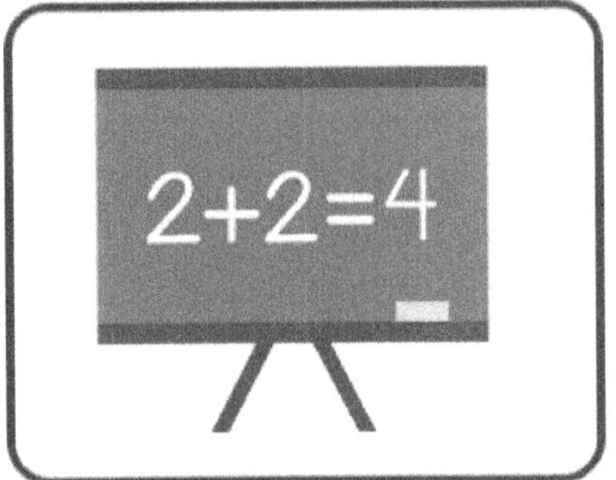

Find the answer to the equation.

usually

Usually I have coffee.

able

Are you able to ride a bike?

teacher

The teacher read to them.

observe

Do you want to observe the stars?

my

My favorite color is blue.

came

He came to class.

temperature

What's the temperature?

truck

Is thaty our truck?

practice

They were at practice.

boat

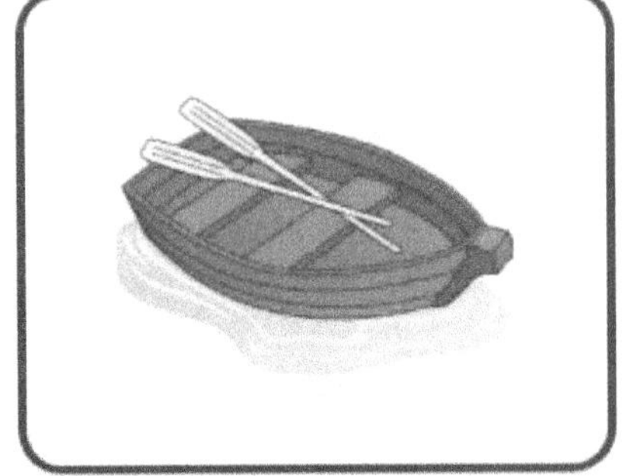

Did you want to go on the boat?

decided

We decided to go to the lake.

door

The door was open.

grew

The flower grew.

pretty

Pretty in pink.

process

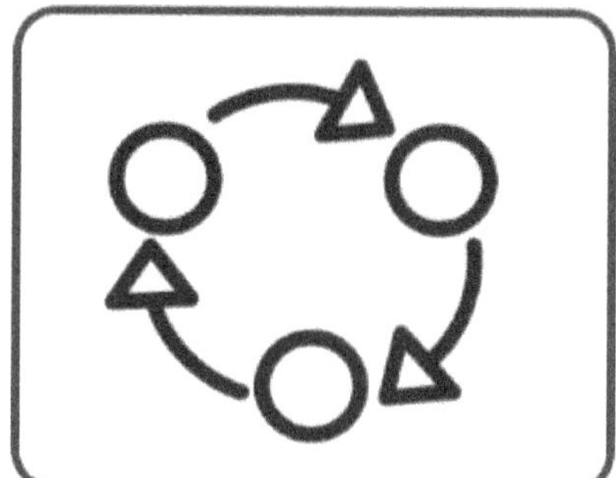

Is that the process?

as

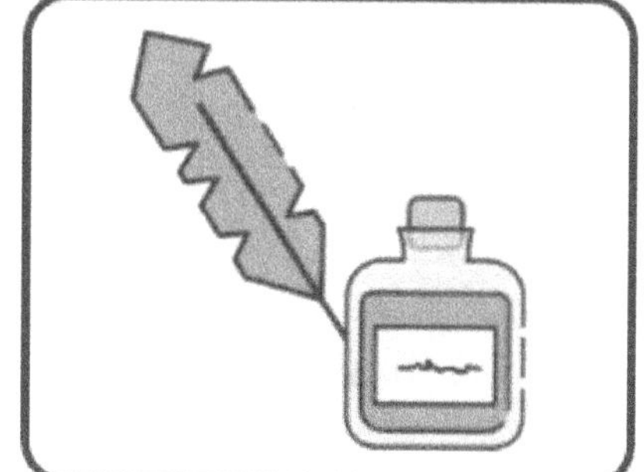

It's light as a feather.

want

I want to ride my bike.

means

She got her by means of a taxi.

top

We put a cherry on top.

voice

Use your quiet voice.

while

We had fun while skiing.

deep

The ocean is very deep.

another

Have another cookie.

head

He wore a cap on his head.

size

What's your shoe size?

us

She taught us.

help

You should help others.

wouldn't

Wouldn't you like to go shopping?

they

They were jump roping.

week

This week is busy.

born

Where were you born?

wall

She painted the wall.

inches

How many inches is it?

set

Please set the table.

isn't

Isn't it nice to hang out with friends?

angle

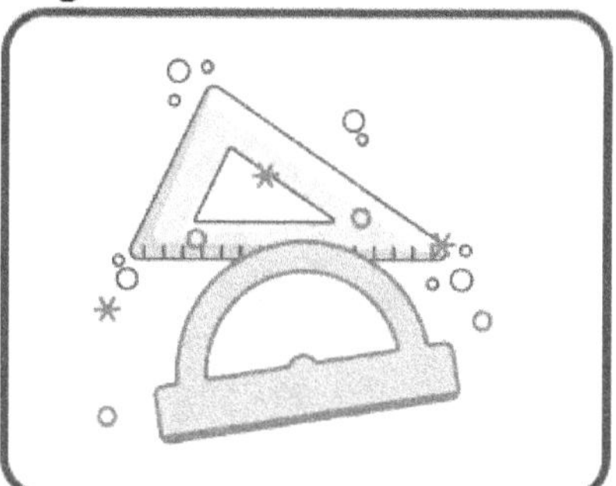

Please measure the angle.

method

We use the scientific method.

were

We were at the carnival.

remain

Please remain in your seat.

especially

She especially liked writing.

type

What type of project is it?

express

They have express delivery.

where

Where do you want to go?

burning

The candles were burning.

window

Plants are in the window.

each

They were one dollar each.

put

Please put the supplies away.

guess

Guess how many

free

They set the tiger free.

lie

It's never good to lie.

carefully

Handle those carefully.

hole

Did you get a hole-in-one?

root

Which team do you root for?

him

John sat next to him.

stick

It's your hockey stick.

gold

She had a gold star.

young

Her kids are young.

current

Are these your current goals?

minutes

How many minutes left?

park

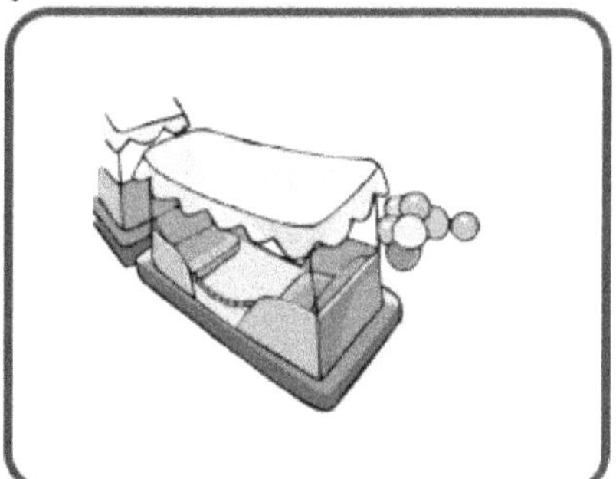

Let's go to the park.

supply

Did you supply what you needed?

point

Point the way.

distance

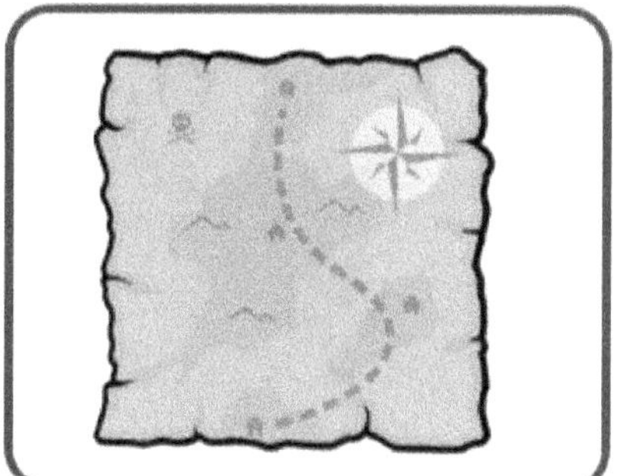

What's the distance to there?

poem

Would you read your poem?

hoe

Use a hoe in the garden.

cost

They cut the cost.

short

You cut your hair short.

hours

How many hours is it open?

summer

Are you ready for summer?

caught

You caught a fish.

force

We learned about force.

paper

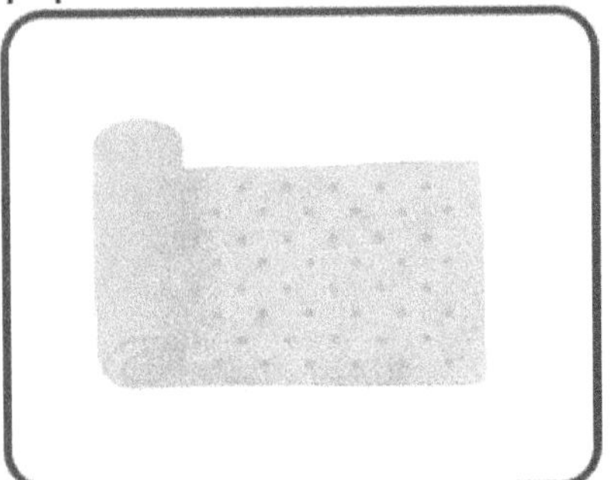

Do you have paper towels?

among

He was among the chairs.

entered

She entered the room.

produce

It will produce vegetables.

sat

They sat and listened.

tied

Did you tie a knot?

cloud

We watched the storm cloud.

perhaps

Perhaps you want to go in it?

piece

This piece fits.

sum

What is the sum of this?

length

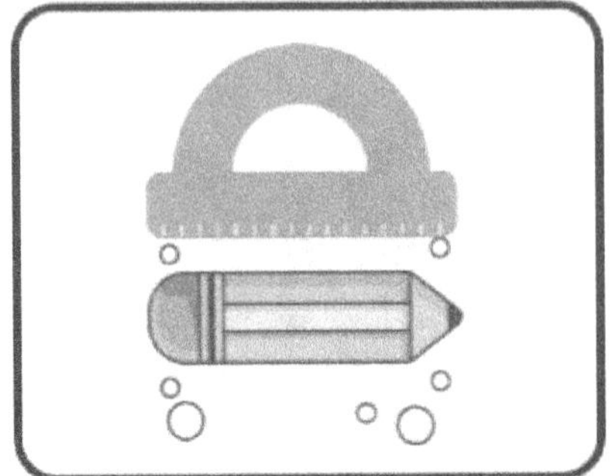

What's the length?

belong

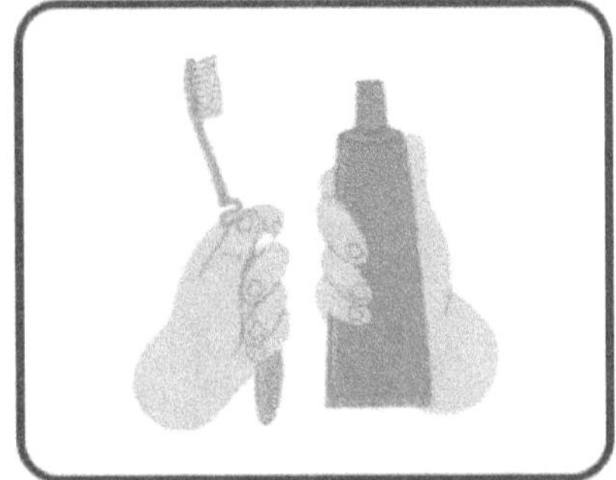

They belong together.

line

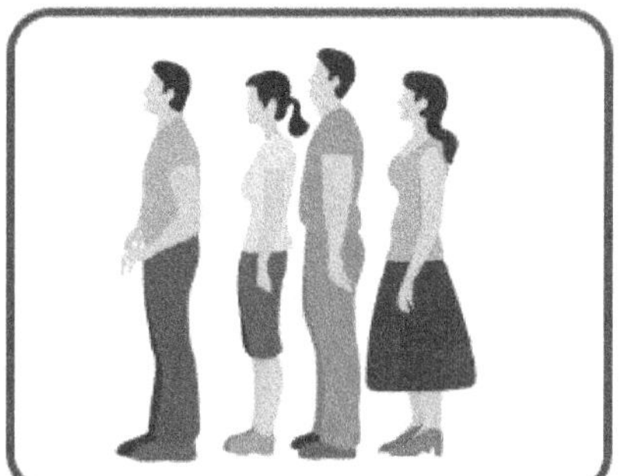

Please form a line.

feet

Put socks on your feet.

dog

My dog is cute.

for

We ate turkey for Thanksgiving.

million

She watched a million how-to videos.

mark

I used a check mark.

return

They were excited to return.

rock

A diamond is part of a rock.

less

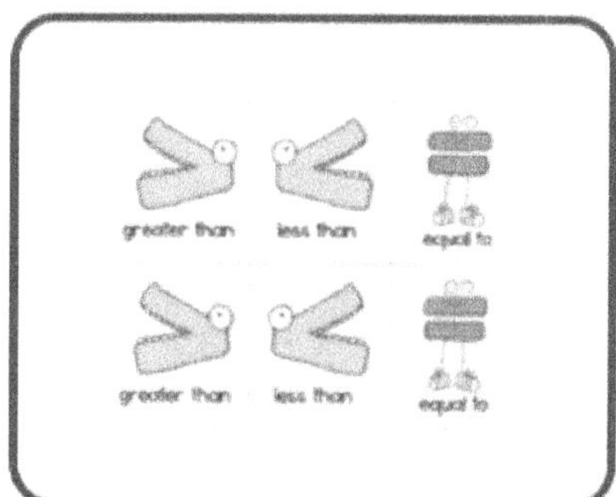

Three is less than five.

their

They liked their teacher.

give

I like to give gifts.

high

She wore high heels.

eat

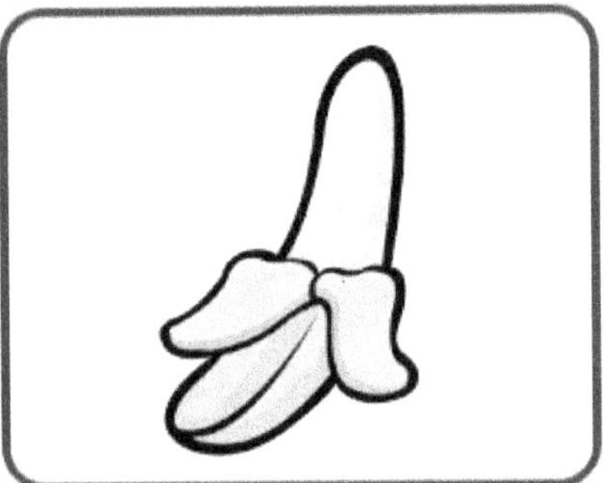

I eat bananas.

probably

It's probably on the list.

blow

Did you blow the bubbles?

toward

She taught toward the front.

plant

I will water the plant.

if

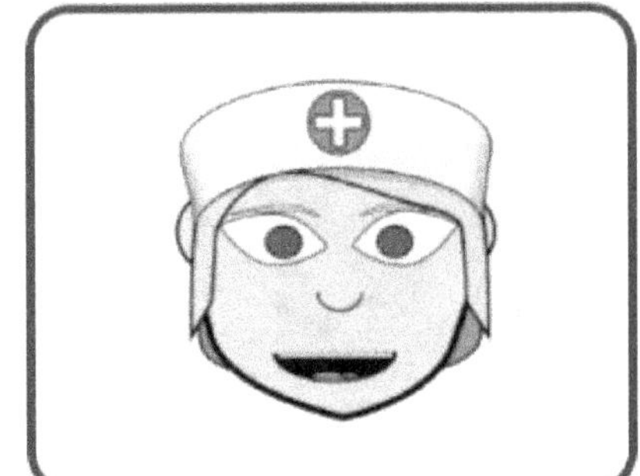

If you are sick, go see the nurse.

industry

This is where the industry is.

doesn't

Doesn't it sound beautiful?

whole

Were you sick the whole time?

like

Do you like to read?

music

I love music.

century

They said it's a century old.

once

Once upon a time…

workers

The workers were busy.

being

She is being shy.

carry

She had a bag to carry her groceries.

light

The light turned yellow.

might

It might rain today.

follow

Follow the teacher.

religion

What religion is it?

cows

How many cows does he have?

dance

They dance like professionals.

natural

This place has natural beauty.

spell

Please spell the word.

got

She got a hair cut.

rich

I want to be rich.

power

What super power do you have?

money

How much money have you saved?

view

That is a beautiful view!

per

It's forty dollars per car.

so

We had so much fun.

song

We will sing a song.

correct

Was that the correct piece?

machine

It's grandma's sewing machine.

ears

Did you get your ears pierced?

material

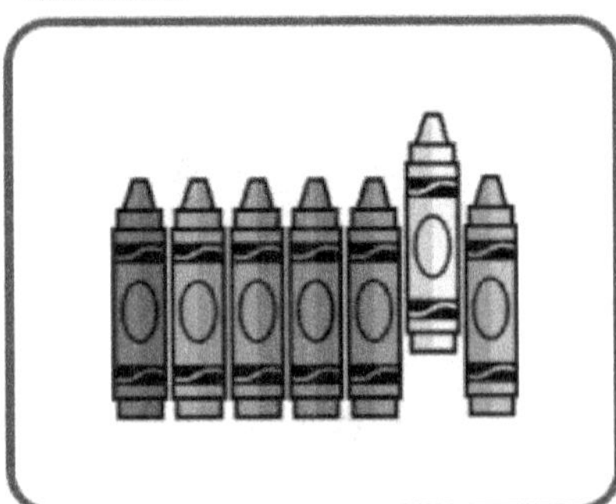

She needed material.

back

We went back to school.

cross

There's a cross on the church.

provide

We wanted to provide food.

me

Come with me to the park.

send

Did you send the letter?

pushed

She pushed the stroller.

located

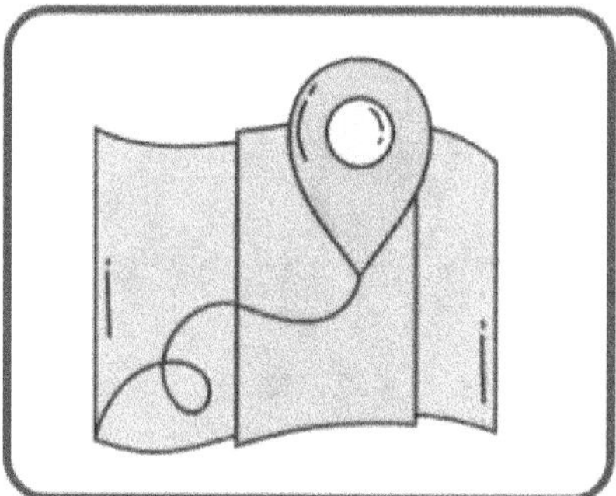

Where is the store located?

syllables

We are working on syllables.

baby

Is this your baby?

sister

Is she your sister?

cat

I adopted a cat.

corner

Turn at that corner.

itself

The house won't clean itself.

out

Take the dog out for a walk.

broken

Her heart is broken.

make

We will make dinner.

dress

She loved her new dress.

real

Her real name is Sally.

major

What's your college major?

ride

Let's ride bikes!

law

It's the law.

ahead

Who was ahead in the race?

could

Could you see the moon?

lot

The car lot was full.

feel

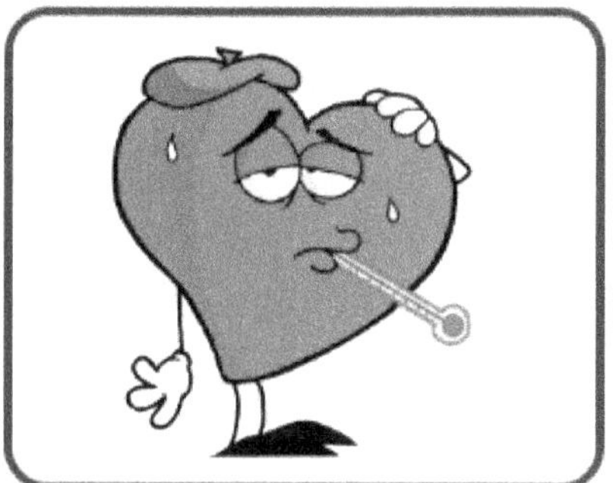

How do you feel?

create

What art did you create?

language

Do you know sign language?

scientists

They are scientists.

kind

Be kind to each other.

shouted

The cheerleaders shouted their cheer.

separate

The brain has separate parts.

modern

She loves modern art.

two

There are two owls.

glass

Did you clean the glass?

building

I made a building with legos.

led

The dog led her.

again

May we go on the ride again?

gun

We played with a water gun.

nation

Which nation are you from?

world

I want to travel the world.

heat

Please heat up the oven.

seven

She has seven lipsticks.

let

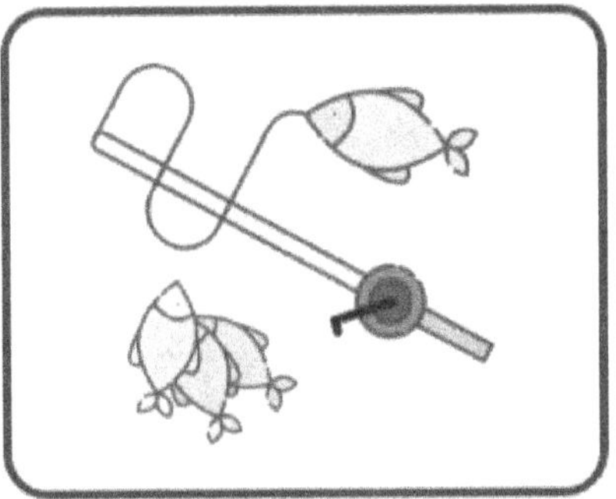

Will you let me go fishing?

care

She'll care for him.

study

It's time to study.

compound

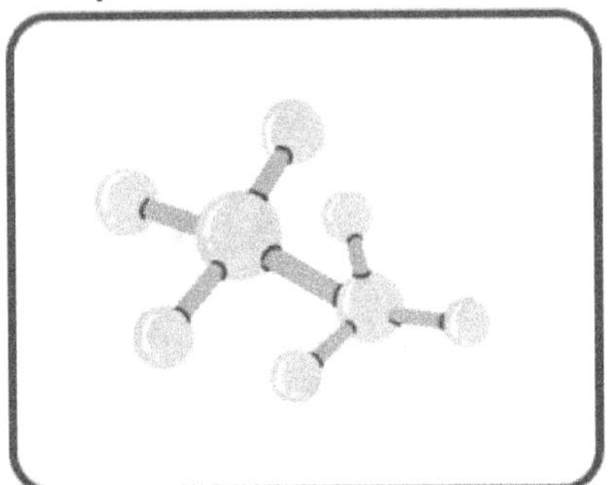

This is a compound.

figure

Who was able to figure it out?

break

Time for a break.

drawing

Is that your drawing?

picture

They took their picture.

raised

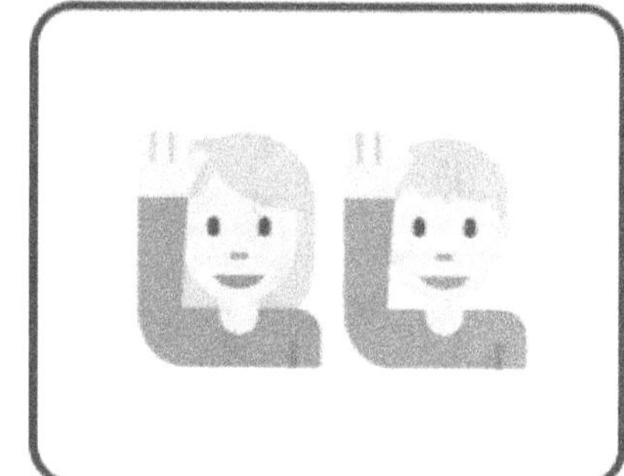

Everybody raised their hands.

yet

Are we there yet?

plains

The road went through the plains

your

Your ball is here.

enjoy

Did you enjoy your coffee?

thus

I was tired, thus I didn't go to the party.

since

Since you like cookies, let's make some.

famous

She's a famous actress.

allow

Did the teacher allow him to go play?

tall

How tall is a giraffe?

couldn't

Couldn't we throw a fundraiser?

various

I watch various shows.

would

Would you like some juice?

took

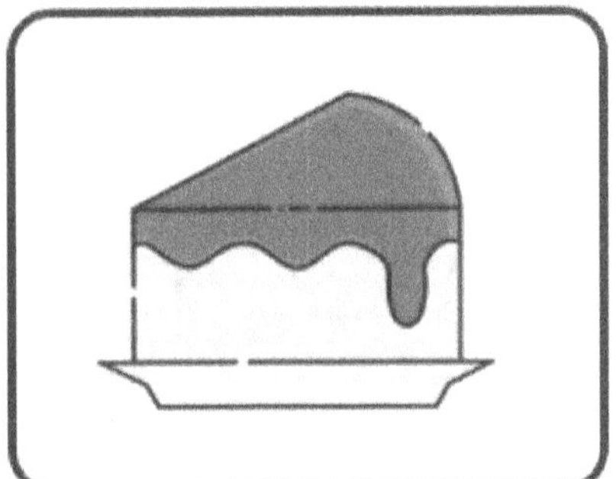

He took the last piece.

chart

What does your medical chart say?

sky

The sky is clear.

shoulder

Did you hurt your shoulder?

just

The train just left.

western

It's western wear day.

what

What is your question?

all

It's all gone!

covered

Snow covered the car.

together

They went shopping together.

bring

Bring your friends!

match

Did you match them?

explain

Please explain it again.

sense

What sense did you just use?

few

She wanted a few more minutes.

son

Is that your son?

ready

Is it ready?

any

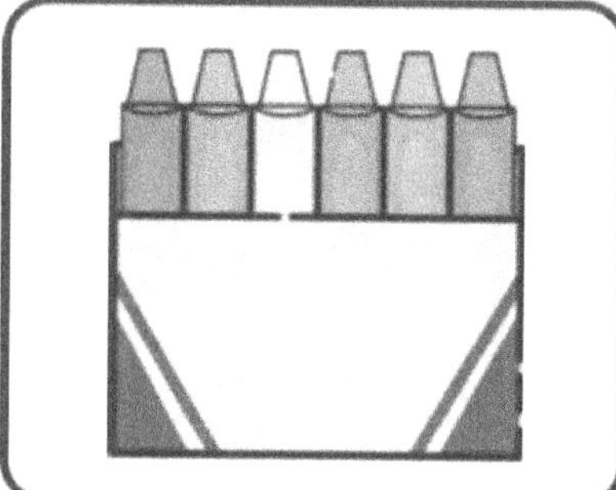

Do you have any crayons?

within

What did you see within the museum.

i'll

I'll call.

can't

When I can't sleep, I count sheep.

bear

He loves his old teddy bear.

by

John sat by Jane.

children

Four children sang.

school

Do you like school?

sir

Yes, sir!

jumped

The cow jumped over the moon.

last

It's the last day of school.

not

A giraffe is not short.

iron

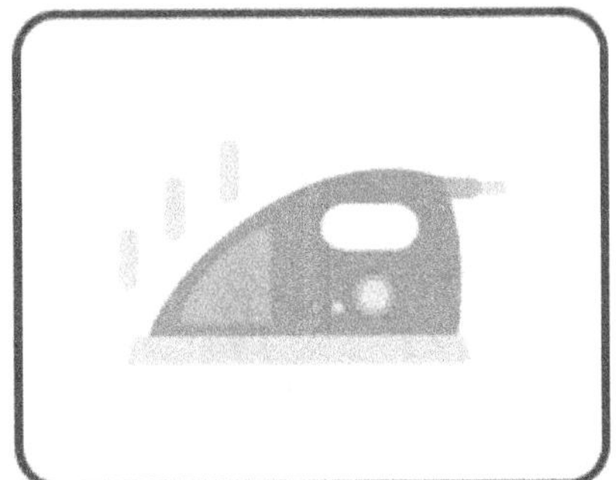

I need to iron my shirt.

steel

The new building used steel.

edge

I stood at the edge of the pond.

sleep

It's time to sleep.

are

We are friends.

state

Which state do you live in?

stop

Do you see the stop sign?

far

How far is it?

eggs

Do you have enough eggs?

whose

Whose guitar is it?

love

Families love each other.

cold

It's cold outside.

elements

Look at the periodic table of elements.

open

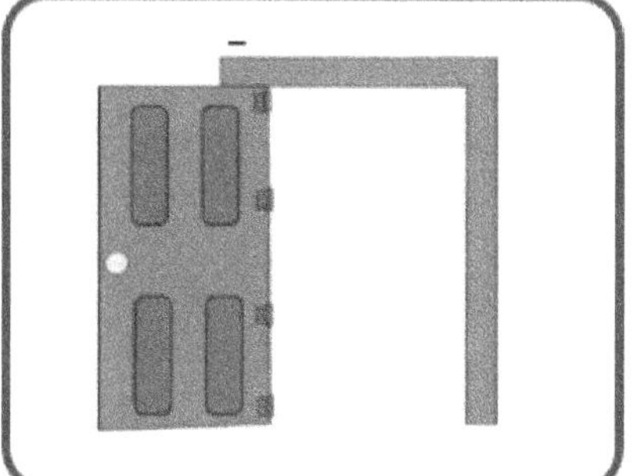

The door is open.

contain

What stories does it contain?

rose

Thank you for the rose.

become

It will become a butterfly.

stars

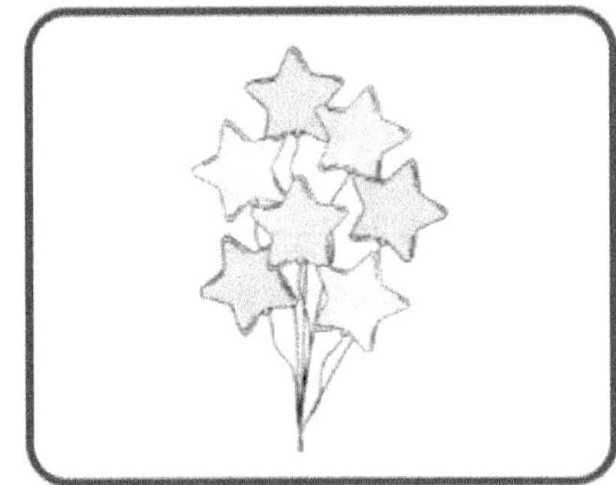

How many stars did you earn?

seem

You seem busy.

scale

Use the scale to weigh them.

tell

She wanted to tell a secret.

indicate

Did you indicate that you are ill?

climbed

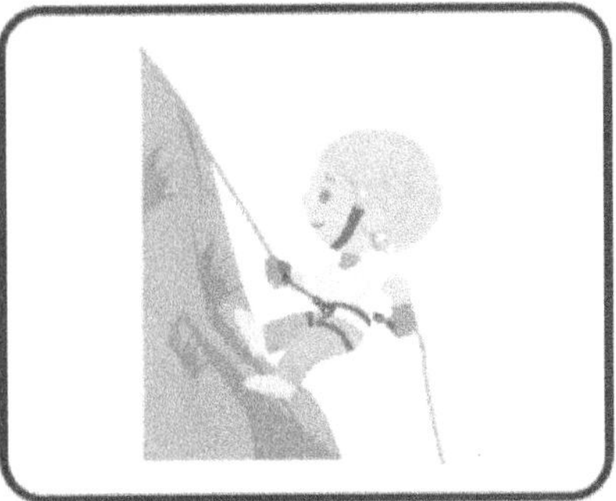

They climbed it.

box

What's in the box?

southern

She's a southern belle.

road

Is this the right road?

visit

They went to visit their grandparents.

strong

How strong are you?

wood

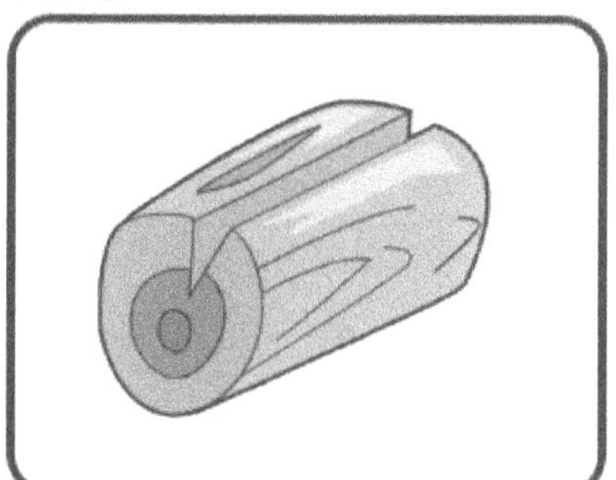

Did you chop the wood?

story

What's the story about?

went

We went to recess.

sit

She decided to sit.

english

Do you enjoy English class?

with

He had toast with his cereal.

five

There are five of them.

soft

The teddy bear is so soft.

letter

He mailed a letter.

listen

Do you listen to music?

fall

Be careful to not fall.

car

He bought a new car.

he

he waved hello.

instead

Do you drink tea instead of coffee?

lady

The lady worked long hours.

space

The astronaut went to space.

wrong

Did I get it wrong?

his

It's his soccer ball.

chance

Dice is a game of chance.

ask

It's good to ask questions.

old

Those are old toys.

yourself

Did you go hiking by yourself?

nose

My nose is running.

paint

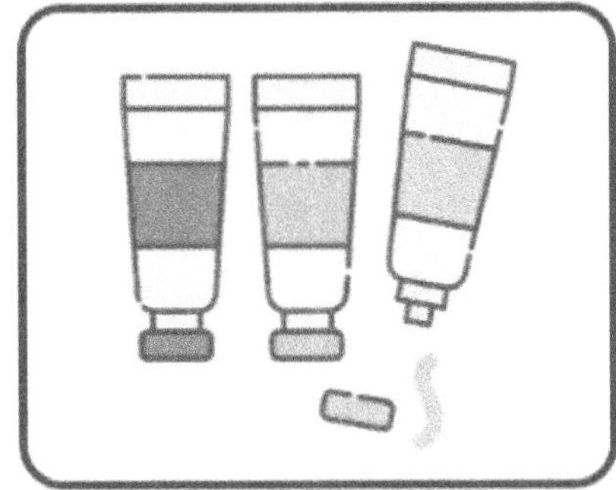

What did you paint?

spread

Spread your wings.

agreed

They agreed on music.

conditions

What are the weather conditions.

get

Did you get your report card?

map

Did you look at the map?

mall

Do you want to go to the mall?

side

Each side of a square is the same.

around

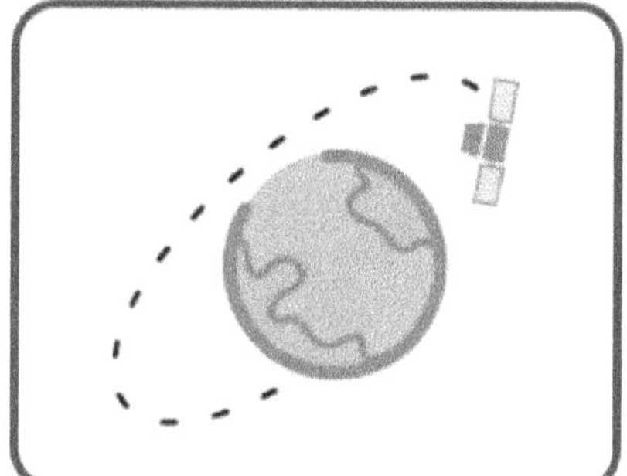

Let's travel around the world

team

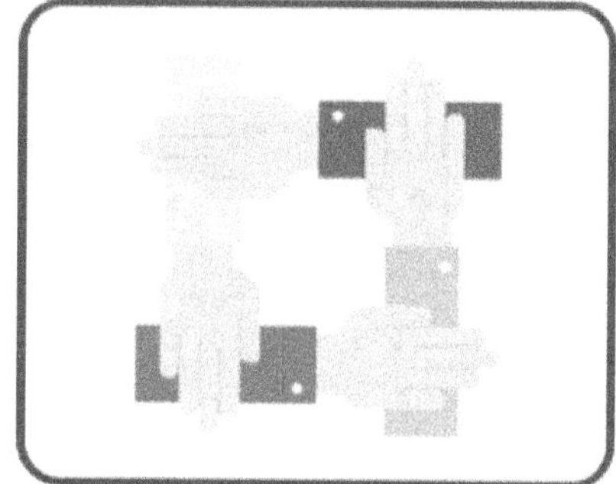

Are you on the basketball team?

those

Those are great cookies!

wire

This telephone has a wire.

better

Feel better soon!

discovered

Who discovered antibiotics?

england

I want to go to England.

gone

Has he gone fishing?

sell

She is going to sell lemonade.

years

You are five years old today.

ago

It happened a long time ago.

though

Even though she's busy, she read alot.

wonder

I wonder what we'll see!

direction

Which direction do we go?

this

This is your backpack.

moon

The wolf howled at the moon.

months

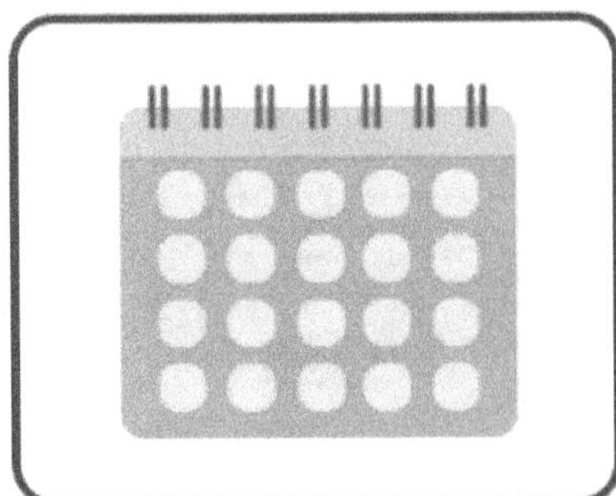

There are several cold months.

watch

Do you wear a watch?

held

They held hands.

was

She was reading.

thought

I thought the novel was good.

silent

Please be silent in the library.

direct

Did you direct the film?

such

He is such a good dog.

stretched

We stretched before the workout.

count

How high can you count?

an

I have an idea!

well

You did well.

other

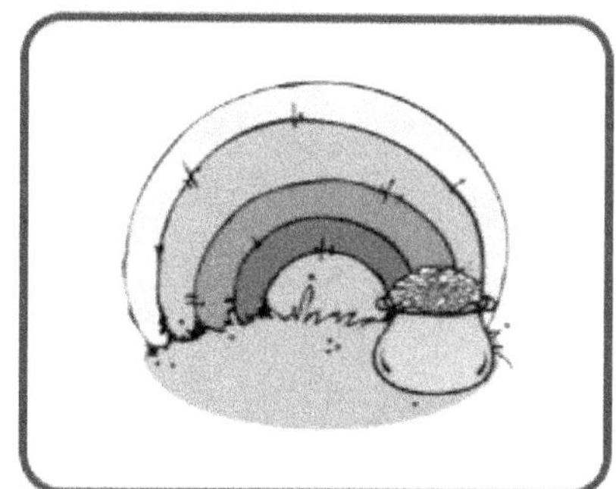

What other colors do we need?

written

It was written down.

rain

It started to rain.

than

He is taller than her.

sea

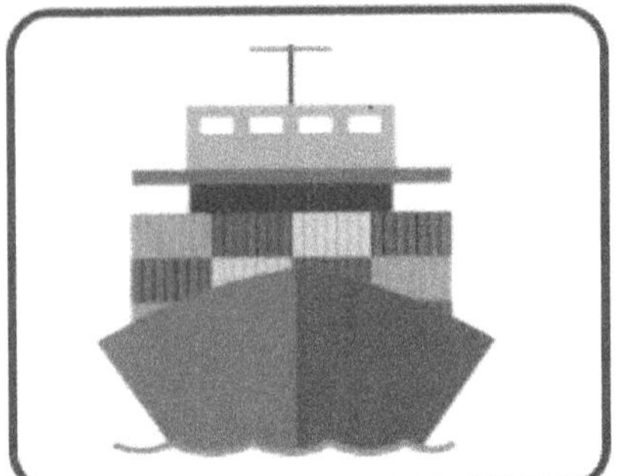

The ship is at sea.

control

Who has the remote control?

is

It is hot outside

cause

What's the cause?

washington

She is from Washington.

has

Lily has a cat.

base

Do you play first base?

don't

Don't forget!

built

He built a house.

describe

Describe the colors.

stood

He stood at the teacher's desk.

half

I hate half the orange.

house

The doll house was pink.

sing

We sing.

how

How was the football game?

stand

Please stand up.

small

The ladybug is small.

beautiful

The area is beautiful.

anything

Do cows eat anything but grass?

suggested

I suggested you do your homework.

walk

We went for a walk.

office

Do you need any office supplies?

effect

How did the medicine effect your cold?

next

Take the next step.

least

Did you at least remember your bag?

without

I can't go without my backpack.

already

I already bought groceries.

man

The man drove.

clothes

Did you hang your clothes up?

design

Did you design this?

try

Try again, please.

symbols

What do those symbols mean?

table

Please sit at the table.

middle

She stood in the middle.

subject

What is your favorite subject?

prepared

She prepared for the exam.

feeling

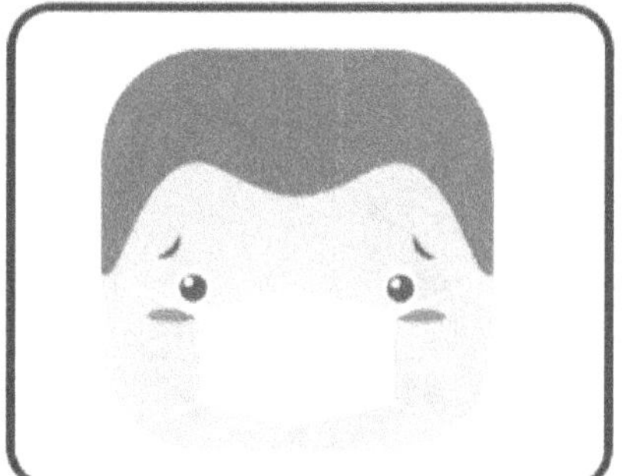

He's feeling sick.

shop

I'm need to go shop for groceries.

lay

Will she lay an egg?

general

We shopped at the general store.

fig

I ate a fig.

brown

It's a brown cow.

hat

I like your new hat.

into

That goes into the bin.

tools

May I borrow your tools?

section

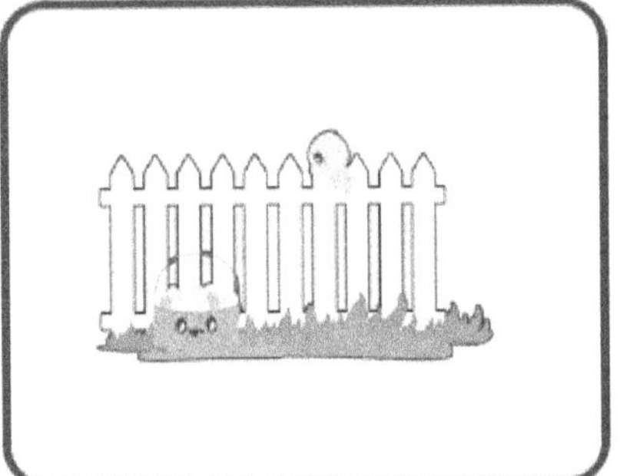

This section is fenced off

long

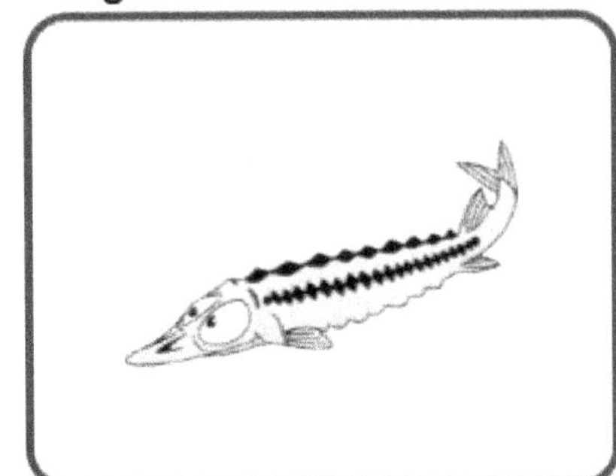

How long is it?

cents

That's just my two cents.

eyes

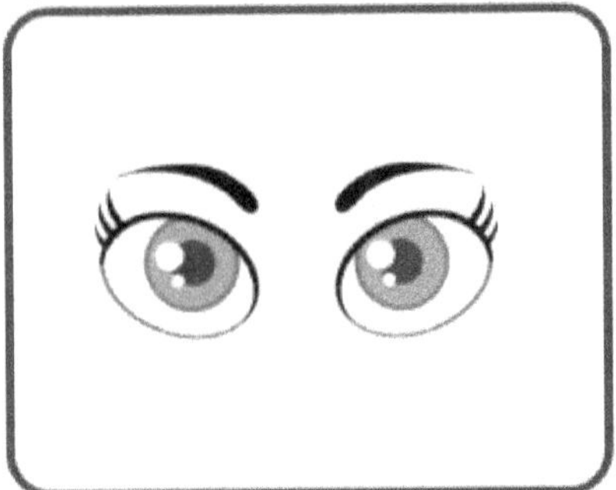

What color are her eyes?

until

I work until 5 o'clock.

ball

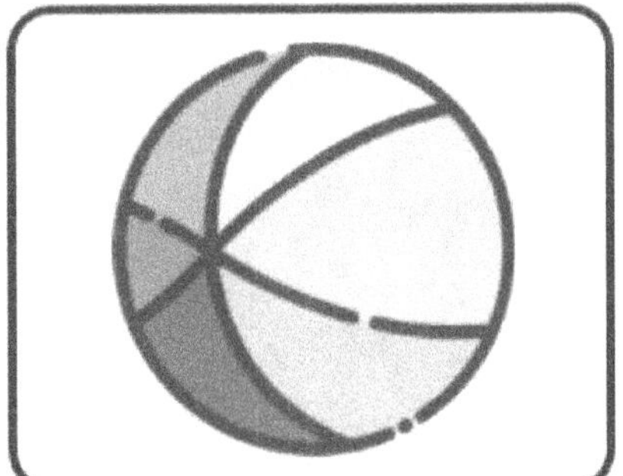

He was among the chairs.

book

I'm reading this book.

farm

They have cows on the farm.

huge

Those trees are huge!

fun

They had fun at the beach

movement

Movement is important.

sand

They played in the sand.

mother

He loves his mother.

fruit

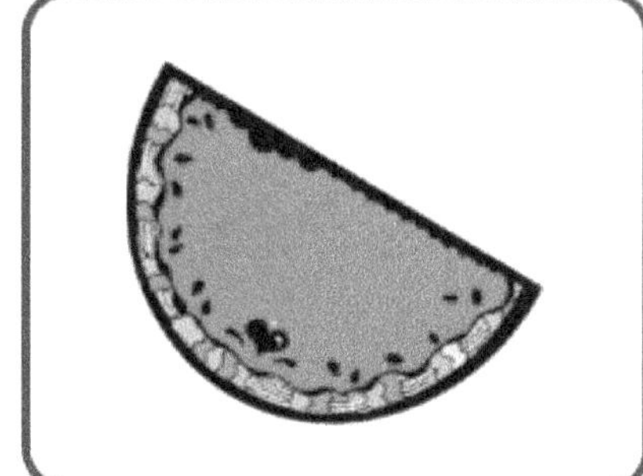

Watermelon is my favorite fruit.

important

It's important!

enough

Did you eat enough pancakes?

government

We learned about the government.

will

I will go to the park.

keep

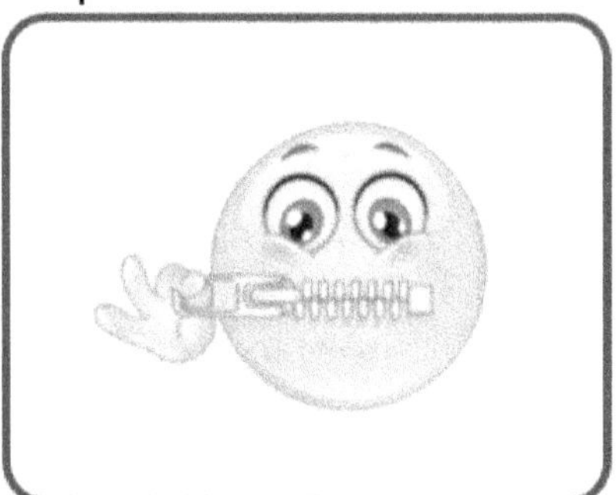

Can you keep a secret?

something

Did you hear something?

then

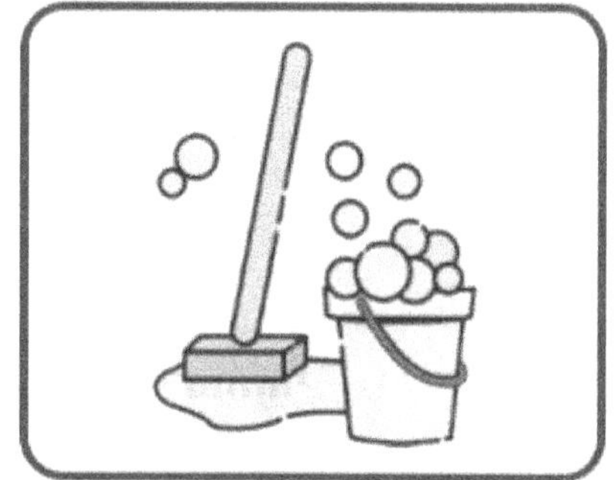

Do your chores, then you can play.

grow

The plant began to grow.

add

If you add one plus two, you get three.

capital

The capital is in Washington DC.

form

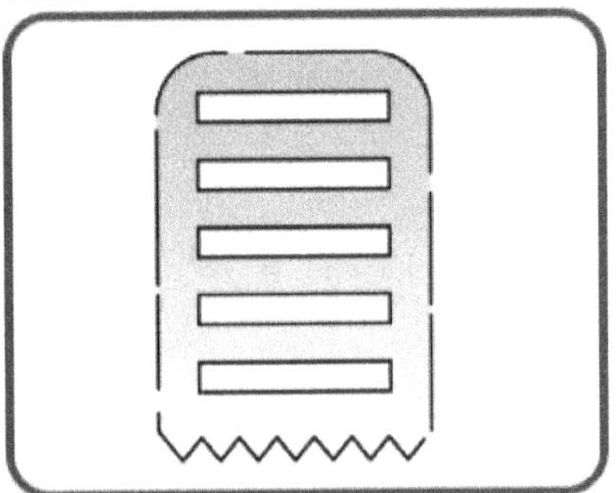

Complete the form.

told

I told you I made a snowman.

trouble

Did you have car trouble?

africa

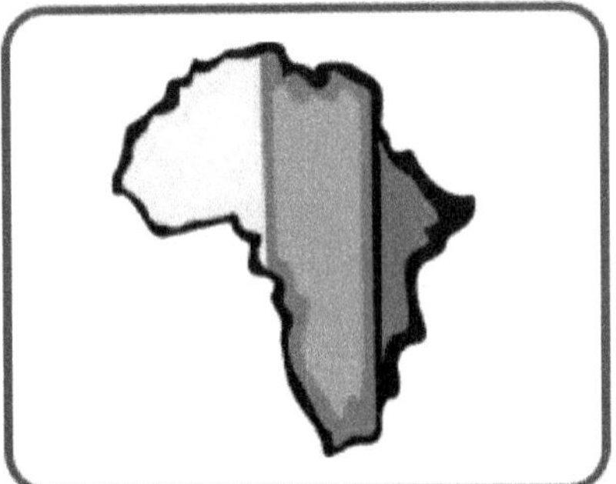

Did you vist Southern Africa?

ice

The ice was melting.

true

It's true love.

received

She received an award.

between

Two is between one and three.

quite

You are quite busy

slowly

The turtle walked slowly.

idea

I have an idea!

night

You can see the stars at night.

early

She had to get up early.

verb

Which word is a verb?

wild

What is your favorite wild animal?

Sample for this book

one

The panda says one.

one one

one

our

This is our room.

our our

our

out

He will go out.

out out

out

own

The man owns a computer.

own own

own

Dolch & Fry Sight Words : Read Trace Write Handbook

a

This is a bird.

a a

a

I

I will play with the toys.

am

I am crawling on the ground.

am am

am

an

This is an ant.

an an

an

as

It is as light as a feather.

as   as
as

at

She is at her friend's house.

at   at
at

be

We will be friends.

be   be
be

by

This story is by me.

by   by
by

Dolch & Fry Sight Words : Read Trace Write Handbook

pig

She is sleeping on her pig.

pig   pig

pig

put

She is putting an arm around her daughter.

put   put

put

ran

She ran back home.

ran   ran

ran

red

The bus is red.

red   red

red

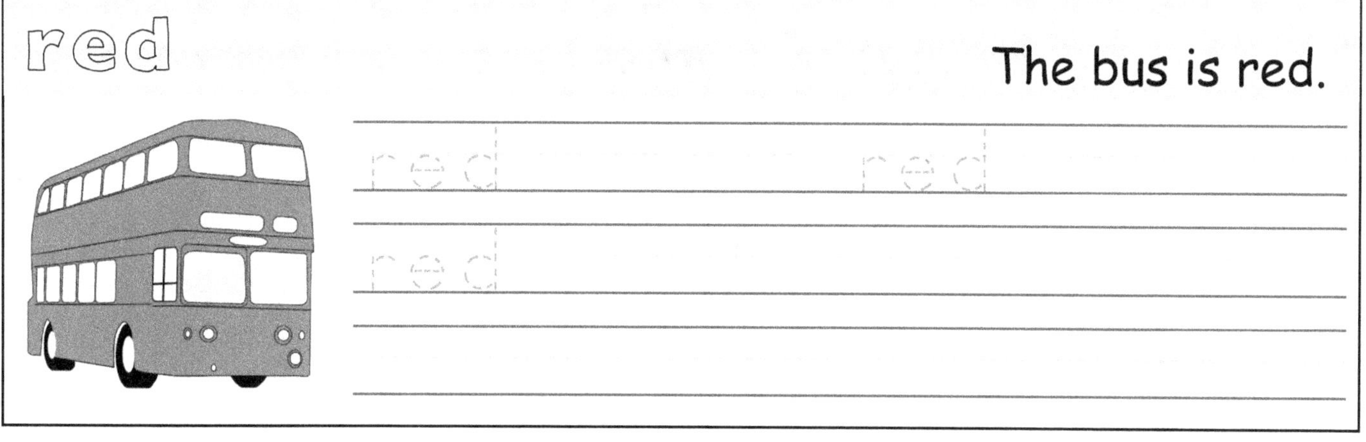

Dolch & Fry Sight Words : Read Trace Write Handbook

do

She will do the cleaning.

do   do

do

go

He will go somewhere.

go   go

go

he

He is bored.

he   he

he

if

If I put my clothes here, it will get washed.

if   if

if

Dolch & Fry Sight Words : Read Trace Write Handbook

in

The baby is in the bath.

in

in

is

The cat is happy.

is

is

it

It is my toy.

it

it

me

It's me.

me

me

my

This is my nose.

my my

my

no

No, I will not!

no no

no

of

One of the boys is my son.

of of

of

on

He turns on the light.

on on

on

or

Should I eat this or that?

or or
or

so

This is so yummy.

so so
so

to

She will read to the end.

to to
to

up

He stacks the blocks upper.

up up
up

us

Both of us are walking.

us   us

us

we

We are helping to make a house.

we   we

we

all

We are all dancing together.

all   all

all

and

My brother and I are playing.

and   and

and

any

They can read any books.

any   any

any

are

The eggs are colorful.

are   are

are

ask

The girl asks a question.

ask   ask

ask

ate

They ate yummy ice cream.

ate   ate

ate

bed

This bed is for the baby.

bed   bed

bed

big

The bottle is huge.

big   big

big

box

The box has all my toys.

box   box

box

boy

The boy is hiding behind it.

boy   boy

boy

but

I want to go, but my son doesn't.

but   but
but

buy

He buys lots of stuff.

buy   buy
buy

can

The baby will drink milk from the can.

can   can
can

car

The car is red.

car   car
car

Dolch & Fry Sight Words : Read Trace Write Handbook

not

She is not feeling well.

not not
not

now

Now I am doing my homework.

now now
now

off

They cut off the paper.

off off
off

old

You are one year old!

old old
old

cat

The cat is sad.

cat   cat

cat

cow

The cow is funny.

cow   cow

cow

cut

They are cutting out paper.

cut   cut

cut

day

This day is the 30th.

day   day

day

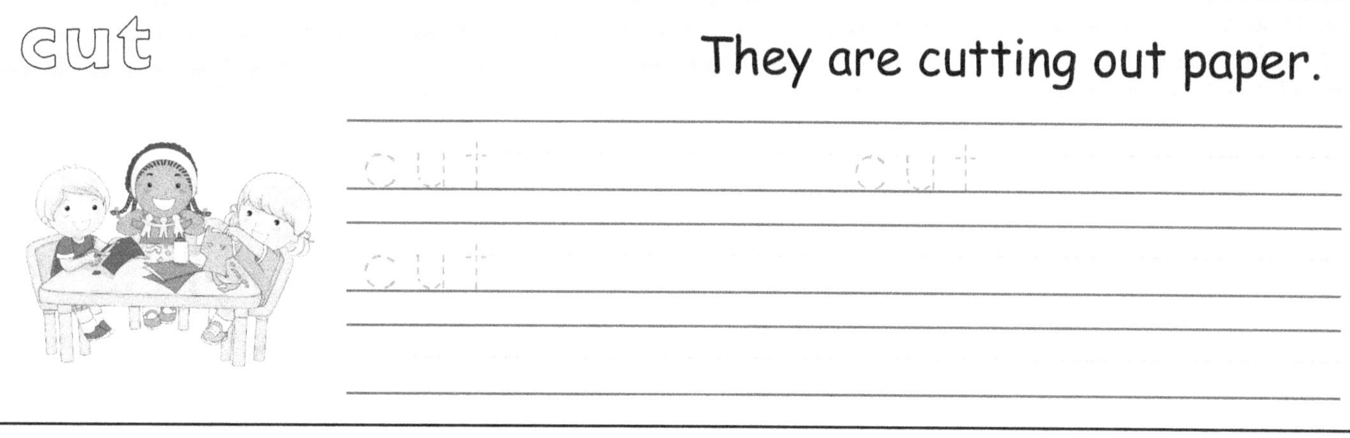

Dolch & Fry Sight Words : Read Trace Write Handbook

her

She has her trolley.

her   her

her

him

I gave my hat to him.

him   him

him

his

His cheeks are big.

his   his

his

hot

It is hot on the beach.

hot   hot

hot

Dolch & Fry Sight Words : Read Trace Write Handbook

man

man   man

man

The man is a vet.

may

may   may

may

May I have more?

men

men   men

men

The men are mining for gold.

new

new   new

new

She has a new hat.

eye

The fox is closing his eyes.

eye   eye

eye

far

He can fly the plane very far.

far   far

far

fly

The bee will fly back home.

fly   fly

fly

for

The dog is begging for food.

for   for

for

get

He will get a trophy.

get　　　get
get

got

The baby got some new toys.

got　　　got
got

had

He had a big tummy.

had　　　had
had

has

She has a doll.

has　　　has
has

how

How many blocks are there?

how   how

how

its

Its legs are short.

its   its

its

leg

His legs are short.

leg   leg

leg

let

Let me come in!

let   let

let

did

She did a great job.

did did

dog

The dog is adorable.

dog dog

eat

The monkey will eat the banana.

eat eat

egg

The egg is small.

egg egg